JOSÉ ORTEGA Y GASSET

BORN IN Madrid in 1883, José Ortega y Gasset was one of the intellectual leaders of the Spanish Republican government. After the establishment of the Republic, Ortega became a member of Parliament. He also held for many years the chair of metaphysics at the University of Madrid and was editor of the influential journal of opinion, *Revista de Occidente*. After the Spanish Civil War, Ortega became an exile from Spain, living for a time in Buenos Aires, later settling in Lisbon. In recent years he visited Spain to lecture in Madrid. *Man and Crisis* was originally published in Spanish under the title of *En Torno A Galileo*. Other books by Ortega include his most widely read work *The Revolt of the Masses*, *Man and People*, *Meditations on Quixote*, *History as a System*, and *What Is Philosophy?* Señor Ortega died in 1955.

"Ortega y Gasset, after Nietzsche, is perhaps the greatest 'European' writer."

—Albert Camus

by JOSÉ ORTEGA Y GASSET

JOSE ORTEGA Y GASSET

WHAT IS
PHILOSOPHY?

TRANSLATED FROM THE SPANISH BY
MILDRED ADAMS

W · W · NORTON & COMPANY

New York · London

W. W. Norton & Company, Inc.
500 Fifth Avenue, New York, N.Y. 10110
www.wwnorton.com

W. W. Norton & Company Ltd.
Castle House, 75/76 Wells Street, London W1T 3QT

Books That Live

The Norton imprint on a book means that in the publisher's
estimation it is a book not for a single season but for the years.
W. W. Norton & Company, Inc.

ISBN 0-393-00126-1

PRINTED IN THE UNITED STATES OF AMERICA

4 5 6 7 8 9 0

Contents

Translator's Preface

IT IS one of the curious paradoxes of Ortega's distinguished career that in his own work he was so seldom a writer of books as books. The son of a newspaper publisher, cradled, as he used to say, on a rotary press, he acted in his early days as a writer of short newspaper essays. After becoming established as a professor of metaphysics, and also as publisher and editor of one of Europe's most distinguished magazines (*La Revista de Occidente*) he wrote longer essays, introductions to other peoples' books, and lectures which he intended to put into book form but was seldom quite ready to hand over to the printer. Pressed to yield for translation and American publication one group of essays which had set Madrid by the ears, or another which had created a sensation in Buenos Aires, he was polite, but not convinced. At the best, he would promise them for an indefinite future date. At the worst, he would take refuge in the uncertainties of the post, and fail to answer.

Ortega's most devoted and articulate disciple, Julián Marías, says that the philosopher excused this behavior on the ground that the essays or the lectures needed changes, but that before completing them his attention would be diverted by something else, and he would be off, like his favorite symbol the gerfalcon, after another ideological quarry.

The result is that only now, since his death in 1955, is

it becoming possible for readers outside of Spain to enjoy and assess the full scope of Ortega's contribution to twentieth-century thought. Even Spaniards, who had the advantage of what his publishers in Madrid called too early his *Complete Works* (*Obras Completas*), find that the posthumous works now being published add substantial and important dimensions to his image and his reputation.

It is one of the distinctions of José Ortega y Gasset, journalist, editor, educator, and philosopher, one of the marks of his greatness, that despite the lag between thought and formal publication which, in a writer less profound, might well render his work frayed by time, the work continues to seem fresh and modern, though years have passed since it was first created. *The Revolt of the Masses*, his most famous book thus far, though first published in English in 1932, grows rather more than less illuminating as the years go by. Its twentieth edition in the United States coincided with the rise of African masses, whose behavior is proving not so different as might be expected from that of the European masses of whom Ortega was writing three decades ago.

After the philosopher's death, when his correcting hand was stilled and his son, who succeeded him as head of the Madrid publishing house, could begin to tap the treasure of unpublished manuscripts that were stacked in his book-lined study, his reputation began to put forth new shoots. Posthumous works that have appeared thus far include *Man and People* (*El Hombre y la Gente*) and *Man and Crisis* (*En Torno a Galileo*). *Leibnitz and the idea of Principle*, published in Madrid in 1959, is in the process of translation.

If the book on Leibnitz will prove to be, as his disciples insist, Ortega's most important philosophic work, this present volume is perhaps the one holding most interest for the amateur of philosophy. Like so many of his later works, it represents a course of lectures which, though first given in Buenos Aires in 1928, and repeated with some variations in Madrid in 1929, he had not had time to revise before he died in 1955. The result is that they read like spoken Spanish, that is, like Ortega's spoken Spanish, and in the movement of the prose one can see the eyebrows peak up, the forefinger come down, the mobile face change, the shoulders present the coming paradox in anticipation of the words. Short of being present in the lecture rooms and the theatre where Ortega delivered them (the latter serving as illustration for one of his important points), the next best thing is to read them.

In the process of sorting and comparing the manuscript pages which held these lectures, the Spanish publishers came from time to time on paragraphs which were meant to serve as emendations or changes in the lectures as delivered. These were part of the ceaseless work of rethinking, rephrasing, re-illustrating which was Ortega's lifelong habit. In the scrupulous Spanish text these paragraphs are printed between brackets, but for readers of English more interested in the development of Ortega's thought than in whether this paragraph or that was included in the first delivery or the second, these barriers have mostly been cleared away. One, called "postcript," and appended to chapter III, remains.

In Madrid the lectures were destined for the University, and indeed were begun there, but the University of Madrid was closed by Primo de Rivera's government because of political agitation, and after some difficulty, arrangements were made to take the course elsewhere and open it to the public. This was in the nature of an experiment. The registration fee was thirty pesetas (then $15), cut in half for students. The first public hall, the Sala Rex, proving too small for the enthusiastic audience, the lecturer moved to the Infanta Beatriz Theatre, where he had a resounding success.

The exact course of events is described by the Spanish editors, beginning with a paragraph from Ortega:

"In February of 1929 I began a course in the University of Madrid entitled "What is Philosophy?" The closing of the University for political reasons, and my consequent departure, obliged me to continue them in the profane surroundings of a theatre. As certain Argentinian readers may be interested in the themes developed in this course, I am trying the experiment of publishing the first of these lectures in *La Nación*. I reproduce in these certain things which were said in my lectures to the Friends of Art and to the Faculty of Letters and Philosophy in Buenos Aires."

With this preliminary note there appeared in that newspaper (*La Nación*) in August, September, and November of 1930, under the general title "Why Return to Philosophy?" certain portions of lessons 2 and 3 of the course which we now print in its entirety. Also in Volume V of the *Obras Completas* there came to light another fragment entitled, "Defense of the Theologian confronting the Mystic," which belongs to lesson 5. Lessons 2 to 6 were delivered in the Sala Rex, and those from 7 on, thanks to the growing public, in the Infanta Beatriz Theatre.

The Buenos Aires lectures which the author mentions were two short courses of five and four lectures respectively, in the two places mentioned, under the titles, "What is Our Life?" and "What is Science; What is Philosophy?" respectively, given during the author's second trip to Buenos Aires in the last quarter of 1928. While these courses appear in the author's *Obras Ineditas*, the reader may consult the resumés published in the Anales de la Institución Cultural Española, Volume III, second part, Buenos Aires, 1953, pages 185 to 248.

The varied life of these lectures, some given here, some there, some published in a newspaper, some in scholarly annals, is characteristic. Also it explains their present shape, and the repetition which occurs in them. The Spanish editors, attentive to Ortega's reputation, and knowing his ways of work, must have been torn between the respect they owed to the work of the master and their desire to make a coherent book out of these related sets of lectures. That they succeeded as well as they did in the latter task is a measure of their skill as applied to his genius.

This is no place to dilate on the difficulties of translating Ortega's thought into a simulacrum of his richly allusive and complex style. The task holds a challenge which never loses its power of attraction, and in which Ortega always emerges the winner. For English inadequacies the translator alone is responsible.

Mildred Adams
New York, June 1960

What Is Philosophy?

1

Philosophy Today. The Strange Adventure which Befalls Truths: The Coming of the Truth. Articulation of History with Philosophy.

In matters of art, love, or ideas I think that programs and announcements are of little use. So far as ideas are concerned, meditation on any theme, if positive and honest, inevitably separates him who does the meditating from the opinion prevailing around him, from that which, for reasons more serious than you might now suppose, can be called "public" or "popular" opinion. Every intellectual effort sets us apart from the commonplace, and leads us by hidden and difficult paths to secluded spots where we find ourselves amid unaccustomed thoughts. These are the results of our meditation.

Now the announcement or program anticipates these results, smooths the path ahead, and discloses the end at which they are to be discovered. But, as we shall see, a thought that is separated from the mental road that leads toward it, a thought standing alone and abrupt as an island, is an abstraction in the worst sense of the word, and by the same token is unintelligible. What is to be gained when one begins an investigation by showing the public what he hopes to find at the top of the steep road? Why start a philosophic inquiry at the end?

So I refuse to put the substance of these lectures into the capital letters of a printed program. I propose to begin at the beginning with what may be for you today, as it was for me yesterday, the starting point.

We begin with a well-known fact, namely, the very different public position in which philosophy finds itself in the collective spirit today if compared with the place it occupied in the early part of this century, and by the same token, the different attitude which the philosopher takes toward his own work and his own profession. The first, like every public and external fact, can be demonstrated by means which also are external; for example, by comparing statistically the number of books on philosophy that the public consumes today with the number it absorbed thirty years ago. It is common knowledge that today, in almost every country, more books on philosophic subjects are sold than on literary subjects, and that a growing curiosity concerning the science of ideas can be found wherever one chooses to look.

This curiosity, this eagerness that makes itself felt at very different levels of conscious clarity is composed of two ingredients: the public is beginning to feel a new *need* for ideas, and at the same time to feel in ideas a certain voluptuous pleasure. The combination of these two characteristics is not accidental: we will see later how every essential need which springs from within, rather than coming by chance from without, is accompanied by a certain pleasurable reaction of the senses. Voluptuous delight is the face that happiness wears. And every living creature is happy when he fulfills his destiny, that is, when he realizes himself, when he is being that which in truth he is. For this reason Schlegel, inverting the relationship between pleasure and destiny, said, "We have a genius for what we like." Genius, man's superlative gift for doing something, always carries a look of supreme pleasure. Later, and with ample evidence, we will find ourselves surprised to discover what may now seem only a phrase—that each one's destiny is in turn his greatest delight.

Compared with the times that preceded it, our era apparently has a philosophic destiny; therefore one takes pleasure in philosophizing—in pricking up one's ears as philosophic phrases roll through the public air, or in flocking to the philosopher as to a traveler thought to bring news direct from the other world.

Contrast such a situation with that which ruled a generation or so ago. And in surprising correspondence with that change in the public spirit, we find that today's philosopher faces philosophy in a state of mind which is completely the opposite of that which his colleagues of the earlier generation found productive. So we are going to talk first of why it is that we approach philosophy in a frame of mind so different from that which ruled among yesterday's thinkers.

Starting at this point, we will move steadily ahead toward a goal which I will not now spell out because it would not yet be understood. We will go moving toward it in concentric circles, their radius growing shorter and developing a greater degree of tension each time we swing around, slipping along from the outside of the spiral, cold, abstract, and indifferent, toward a center which is frighteningly intimate, even pathetic in itself, although not in our way of handling it. The great philosophic problems demand a tactic like that which the Hebrews used for the taking of Jericho and its innermost rose gardens: making no direct attack, circling slowly around them, tightening the curve every time and holding live in the air the dramatic sound of trumpets. In an ideological siege it is the dramatic melody which keeps alert the consciousness of those problems that form the drama of ideas.

I hope this tension will not slacken, for the road we are now starting is of such nature that it gains in attraction as we go forward. From the external and the abstruse which we have just mentioned we drop to more immediate matters, the most immediate matters in that they concern our very lives, the lives of each and every one of us. We are going to descend boldly below what each one customarily thinks his life to be and which really is merely its crust; piercing this crust, we will enter into subterranean zones of our own living, zones which hold for us the most intimate secrets of being, secrets of our deepest selves, of the pure being of our being.

But the fact of saying this is, I repeat, by no means an announcement; on the contrary, it is a safeguard and a precaution which I am obliged to take in view of the unexpected abundance of listeners whom our generous and restless city, far more restless than one might think, and restless in a much more essential sense, has sent me. Under the title "What is Philosophy?" I announced an academic course—therefore a strictly scientific course. I do not know whether a misinterpretation of that title made many believe that I was proposing to give an elementary introduction to philosophy, that is, to treat the complex of traditional philosophic question in a superficial and simplified fashion. I must clear away any such error; it could only distract and defraud your attention. What I want to do is the exact opposite of an introduction to philosophy: it is to take the philosophic activity itself, philosophizing itself, and submit it to basic analysis. So far as I know, this, strange as it may seem, has never been done; certainly it has not been done with the degree of resolution which we are now going to apply to it.

Far from being one of these themes that is considered proper for public interest, this is a matter which, in the beginning at least, seems to be of the most technical and professional interest, suitable only for philosophers. If, as we deal with it, we stumble on themes that seem more human, if in the rigorous search for what philosophy may be, we happen suddenly to fall through a trap door into the most human of the human, into the warm and palpitating heart of life itself and there find ourselves pursuing problems of the street, and even of the bed-chamber, this will be because it has to be that way, because the technical development of my technical problem demands it, and not because I advertise problems, hunt for them, or think them out in advance. The only thing I announce is the exact opposite—a monographic study on a hypertechnical question. Therefore I remain free, and at liberty not to renounce any one of the intellectual difficulties imposed by such a proposal.

At the same time I must make the most loyal effort so that what I say will be clear to all of you, even to those who have had no previous training. I have always thought that clarity is the form of courtesy that the philosopher owes; moreover, this discipline of ours considers it more truly a matter of honor today than ever before to be open to all minds and porous for their probing. This is different from the individual sciences which increasingly impose between the treasure of their discoveries and the curiosity of the profane the tremendous dragon of their closed terminology. I think that the philosopher must, for his own purposes, carry methodical strictness to an extreme when he is investigating and pursuing his truths, but when he is ready to enunciate them and to give them out, he ought to avoid the cynical skill with which some scientists, like a Hercules at the fair, amuse themselves by displaying to the public the biceps of their technique.

So I say that for us today philosophy is a very different thing from what it was for the last generation. But to say this is to recognize that truth changes, that yesterday's truth is today's error and that by the same token today's truth will not be serviceable tomorrow. Does this not rob our own truth of prestige? Skepticism's most popular argument, and certainly a rough one, was Agrippa's figure of speech called τὸν ἀπὸ τῆς διαφωνίας τῶν δοξῶν, concerning the lack of consonance among dogmas. The variety and change of opinions about truth, the devotion to doctrines not only different but apparently in contradiction, is such as to invite incredulity. Therefore, let us at this point go forth to meet this popular skepticism.

More than once you will have pondered on the strange adventure which befalls truths. Take, for example, the law of universal gravitation. In the measure in which this law is true there is no doubt that it has always been true, that ever since bodies, ponderable matter, existed they have always behaved according to its formulation. Nevertheless, this law had to wait until a sunny day in the seventeenth century when it was discovered by a man in one of the British isles. And it is not impossible that on another sunny day men may forget this law; not refute it or correct it, because we are assuming its character to be that of complete truth, but simply forget it, and in that respect return to the same state of failing to suspect it that they were in before Newton discovered it.

This frailty gives truths a double condition which is exceedingly curious. In themselves they exist forever, without alteration or modification. Yet their acquisition by a real person, subject to time, gives them an aspect that is historical; they surge forth on one date, and they may disappear on another. Clearly this temporal quality does not affect them, but it does affect their presence in the human mind. What really happens in time is the psychic act with which we think about them; this is a real event, an effective change in the flow of moments. It is the fact of our knowing these truths, or being ignorant of them, which has a history. And it is this which is mysterious and disquieting, for it means that by virtue of one of our thoughts, a transitory and fugitive reality in a most fugitive world, we enter into possession of something that is permanent and supertemporal. Thought, then, is a point where two worlds, antagonistic in composition, come together. Our thoughts are born and die, pass, return, succumb. Meanwhile their content, that which is thought, remains invariable. Two and two continue to be four when the intellectual act with which we understand this truth has ceased to be. But even to say this, to say that truths are always truths, is inadequate. To exist forever, sempiternal existence, means the persistence of something throughout the length of the time series, an unlimited duration which is no less duration than is that of the may-fly; enduring is being submerged in the torrent of time, more or less vulnerable to its influence.

Well then, truths do not last for much or for little time, they do not possess any temporal attribute, they do not bathe in the river of time at all. Leibnitz called them *vérités éternelles,* in my judgment improperly (later we

will see for what basic reasons). If the sempiternal lasts
as long as the totality of time itself, the eternal exists
before time begins and after it ends, but it includes
within itself all of time, it is duration raised to hyperbole,
a superduration. So much is this so that in it duration is
conserved at the same time as it is annulled: an eternal
being lives an infinite time, that is, it lasts for a single
instant, that is to say, it does not last, it "possesses, complete and integral, in a manner both simultaneous and
complete, a life without end." This, in fact, is the delicate
definition of eternity which Boethius gives—*interminabilis
vitae tota simul et perfecta possessio.*

But the relation of truths to time is not positive but
negative, it is simply not having to deal with time in any
sense, it is being completely apart from all temporal
qualification, it is maintaining oneself entirely outside of
time. To say, then, that truths are always true does not,
strictly speaking, involve less impropriety than if we
say—to use a famous example which Leibnitz brought
to another proposition—"green justice." The ideal body
of justice offers no sign nor orifice where the attribute
"greenness" can be hooked onto it, and however many
times we try to insert it we see it slide over justice as
over a polished surface. Our attempt to put both concepts together fails, and even though we speak of them
in the same breath they stay stubbornly apart without
any possible adherence of the one to the other.

There is no greater degree of heterogeneity than that
which exists between the atemporal mode of being which
is characteristic of truths, and the temporal manner of
being that is native to the human being who discovers
truths and thinks them, knows them or ignores them,
repeats them or forgets them. If, however, we use that
phrase, "truths are always true," it is because, speaking

practically, this carries no erroneous consequences. It is an error, but innocent and convenient. Thanks to it, we look at that strange manner of being which truths enjoy in the same time-conscious way with which we customarily look at things in our world. In the last analysis, to say of something that *it is always what it is*, is equivalent to affirming its independence of temporal variations, its lack of vulnerability. Within the temporal sphere this is the characteristic which is closest to the pure nontemporal, it is a quasi-form of the nontemporal, the *species quaedam aeternitatis*.

Hence, Plato, seeing that it was necessary to place truths, which he called Ideas, outside the temporal world, invented another extra-mundane quasi-place, the ὑπενουρανος τόπος, the supercelestial region; although this had serious consequences in Plato's thinking, let us recognize that, as an image, it was fertile. It allows us to represent our temporal world to ourselves as a sphere surrounded by another circumference having a different ontological atmosphere where live the nontemporal truths, indifferent to time. But note that at a certain instant, one of those truths, the law of gravitation, filtered down from that other world into our own, as if taking advantage of a crevice which widened and let it pass. Like a meteorite, the idea is projected into the world of humans and of history—an image of the coming, the descent which throbs in the depth of all religions that acknowledge the existence of a God.

But that fall, that filtering of a transmundane truth into our world, poses an extremely precise and suggestive question which (and this is shameful) still remains to be investigated. The crevice which opened and gave the truth a chance to slip through is no other than the mind of a man. Well now, why is such a truth apprehended, why is it captured on such and such a day by such and such a man, if, like its sister truths, it has pre-existed indifferent to time? Why was it not thought of before, or afterwards? Why was its discoverer not someone else?

Apparently this is a matter of an essential affinity between the figure of that truth and the form of the crevice, the human subject through which it passes. Nothing happens without reason. If what happened was that the law of gravitation was not discovered until Newton came along, it is evident that some affinity must have existed between the human individual, Newton, and that law. What kind of an affinity is this? Is it a likeness? We are not trying to make the question easy, but on the contrary to emphasize its enigmatic force. How can a man resemble a truth—a geometric truth, for example, or any other—in any way? In what does the man Pythagoras resemble the theorem of Pythagoras? The schoolboy, joking, will say that the theorem resembled his breeches, thus showing an unconscious inclination to pair the theorem with the person of its author. The difficulty is that Pythagoras did not wear breeches; in his day they were worn only by the Scythians who, on the other hand, did not discover theorems.

Here, for the first time, we stumble on a basic distinction which differentiates our philosophy from that which has held the stage for centuries. This distinction consists in taking account of something that is very elemental: namely, that there is no direct resemblance between the person who thinks, sees or imagines something and the thing seen or imagined by him; on the contrary, there is a generic difference between them. When I think of the Himalayas, neither I who think nor my act of thinking resembles a Himalayan peak: the peak is a mountain occupying an enormous space, while my thinking has nothing of a mountain about it, nor does it occupy even the smallest space. But the same thing happens if, instead of thinking of the Himalayas, I think of the number eighteen. In my consciousness, my being, my spirit, my subjective self, I do not find anything which might be an eighteen. As a crowning touch, we can say that the act in which I think of eighteen units is itself alone and unique. You tell me if there is likeness between them. These are clearly heterogeneous entities.

And yet the fundamental task of history, if it wishes to be in all seriousness a science, must be to show how this philosophy, or that political system, could only have been discovered, developed, and, in short, lived by a particular type of man who lived at a particular date. Why, among the many possible types of philosophy, was it only "criticism" which came to lodge, to make itself actual, in the soul of Kant? Is it not clear that in order to explain it, to comprehend it, we must build a double table of correspondence wherein each type of objective idea will be counterbalanced by the related subjective state, the type of man capable of thinking it?

But do not fall back into the triviality which has blocked the march of thought for the past eighty years —do not interpret what has been said as if it implied a basic relativism, so that each truth would be true only for a certain person. The fact that a truth, if thus it is, has value for everybody, and the fact that only one or two people—or only in a single period—will come to know it and to lend it their support—these are two completely different things; for the very reason that they are different one must put them together, bring them into harmony, overcome the scandalous situation of thought in which the absolute value of the truth seemed incompatible with the change in opinions which human history shows in such abundance.

We must recognize variations in thinking not as changes in yesterday's truth which convert it into today's error, but as changes in man's orientation which lead him to see other truths that are different from those of yesterday. It is not truths that change, but man who changes and who, because he changes, goes on scanning the series of truths, goes on choosing from that transmundane sphere to which we earlier alluded the ones which are right for him, and blinding himself to all the rest. Note that this is history's basic and fundamental *a priori*. Is it not the history of man?

And what kind of entity is this called man, whose variations throughout time history aspires to investigate? It is not easy to define man; the margin of his differences is enormous; the bigger it is and the broader the concept of man with which the historian begins his labor, the more profound and precise will be his work. Kant is a man, so is the pygmy of New Guinea, or the Australian Neanderthaloid. Nevertheless, between the extreme ends of human variation there must be a minimum ingredient of common characteristics; the margin which we grant humanity in order that it may be humanity must have a limit.

The ancient world and the medieval world each had their minimum definition of man; strictly speaking, and to our shame let it be said, it has not been surpassed: man is the rational animal. We agree with this; the difficulty is that it has become no small problem for us to know clearly what it is to be an animal, and what it is to be rational. Therefore we would rather say, for the uses of history, that man is every living being who thinks with meaning, and whose thinking we are therefore able to understand. The minimum that history assumes is that the subject of whom it speaks can be understood. Well then, a thing or a being cannot be understood unless it possesses some degree of truth. An absolute error would not seem such to us because we would not even understand it. History's profound assumption, then, is the complete opposite of a basic relativism. When history goes to study primitive man it assumes that his culture had meaning and truth, and that if it had these attributes it continues to have them. What if, at first sight, so much that those creatures do and think seems so absurd to us? History is the second look which manages to find the reason for what appears to be un-reason.

Therefore history is not properly history, does not fulfill its inner mission, unless it achieves an under-standing of man in his period, whatever that may be, including the most primitive. But it cannot understand this if man himself in that period leads a life that has no meaning, if what he thinks and does has no rational structure. In this manner history is bound to justify all periods, and this is the opposite of what it was first threatening to be; on showing us the variability of human opinions it seems to condemn us to relativism, but as it gives full meaning to each relative position that man takes, and reveals to us the eternal truth which every period has lived, it overcomes whatever there is in relativism that is incompatible with faith in man's extra-relative and, as it were, eternal destiny. For very concrete reasons, I hope that in our age the curiosity about the eternal and invariable which is philosophy and the curiosity about the inconstant and changing which is history may come together and embrace.

For Descartes, man is a pure rational entity incapable of variation; hence history seems to him to concern the inhuman in man, and he attributes it to the sinful will which is continually making us cease to be rational entities and fall into infrahuman adventure. For him, as for the eighteenth century, history has no positive content, but represents the series of errors and equivocations which man has committed.

On the other hand, the historical theory of the nineteenth century joined with positivism to cut themselves loose from every eternal value in order to salvage the relative value of each separate period. It is useless for us to try to do violence to our modern sensibilities which resist any impulse to dispense with either dimension, the temporal or the eternal. To bring both of them together must be the great philosophic task of the present generation: for this I have managed to initiate a method which the Germans, with their liking for elaborate labels, have baptized for me with the name "perspectivism."

From 1840 to 1900 it can be said that humanity went through one of those periods which are least favorable to philosophy. It was an anti-philosophic age. If philosophy could be abolished, there is no doubt that during those years it would have disappeared completely. However, as it is not possible to root out of the human mind its philosophic bent, what was done was to reduce it to a minimum. And the entire battle—which certainly will still be hard enough—in which we are presently engaged consists in starting anew toward a philosophy which shall be full and complete, toward a maximum of philosophy.

How was that reduction of philosophy, that shrinking of the body of philosophy, brought about? The series of causes which explain so curious a thing will occupy us in the next chapter.

2

Philosophy Contracts and Expands. The Drama of the Generations. The Imperial Triumph of Physics. Pragmatism.

FOR reasons that I need not tell you now, I have had to suspend the public course which I began at the University. As I started it not lightly, but out of a serious and compelling desire to explore new ideas of considerable interest, I thought I ought not to leave that course strangled at birth, and subject to inference more anecdotal than accurate. Hence you find me here, in these very different surroundings.[1]

I must start by reminding you of two points which are essential. The first is that under the title "What is Philosophy?" I do not propose to give you an elementary introduction to that field of learning. Quite the contrary. We are going to take the whole of philosophy, the very process of philosophizing, and subject it to vigorous analysis. Why is it that the world of men includes this strange fauna called philosophers? Why is it that the thoughts of men include those which we call philosophies? As you can see, this is not a theme which could be called popular but one that bristles with technicalities.

---

[1] See Translator's Preface, pp. 9–10. [Translator's note]

Do not forget that this is an academic course, a university course, though somewhat *in partibus infidelium*. By laying out for you the sea path that lies ahead I free myself to touch at all the conceptual headlands which such a project includes. I must manage to make myself clearly understood by all of you, for, as I have said before, I think that clarity is a courtesy which philosophy owes. But in addition, this problem which is so very technical, so hypertechnical, obliges us to put to ourselves technically the least technical problem that exists—the problem of defining and analyzing what "our life" is, in the most immediate and ordinary sense of those terms, including what our life is day by day. Indeed, one of the things which we must define with the greatest formality is the very thing which we call vaguely, "daily life," the day-by-day quality in life.

The second point on which I touched earlier consists in noting that in philosophy a straight line is not usually the shortest road. The great philosophic problems yield to conquest only when they are treated as the Hebrews treated Jericho—by approaching them on a curved path, marching around and around them in concentric circles which become ever tighter and more suggestive. Therefore, all the subjects that we may touch on, even those which at first glance seem somewhat literary, will appear again and again in later circles on a radius which is ever narrower and more demanding. You will often find that what seemed at first to wear the look of a pure phrase or a decorative metaphor will next turn up with the grave face of a stiff and difficult problem.

Over the course of this century the philosopher's attitude toward his own work has changed. I am not now referring to the fact that the doctrinal content of philosophy is different today from what it was in 1900 or

in 1910; before the philosopher can enter into and
elaborate on this doctrinal content he finds himself in
a very different frame of mind from that which the
thinker of an earlier generation met within himself. As
I said earlier, the last sixty years of the nineteenth
century formed one of the periods least favorable to
philosophy. It was an anti-philosophic age. If philosophy
were something that we could entirely dispense with,
there is no doubt that in those years it would have completely disappeared. As it is not possible to tear out of
the human mind, once awake to culture, its philosophic
dimension, what that age did was to reduce it to a
minimum. Now, however, the attitude with which
today's philosopher begins his work includes a clear
desire to sally forth into a philosophy in full sail, complete and entire; in short, a philosophy at the maximum.

And it is natural that, faced with such a change, we
should ask ourselves how that reduction, that shrinking
of the philosophic mind, was brought about, and what
has happened since to expand it anew, to give it renewed faith in itself of such quality that it is prepared
even to take the offensive again. The only adequate way
to clarify these happenings would be by defining the
structure of European man in the two periods. Any
explanation of the visible changes appearing on the
surface of history which does not go deep down until
it touches the mysterious and latent changes produced in
the depths of the human soul is superficial. Like the one
we are about to give for the changes mentioned above,
it may suffice for the limited purpose of our thesis, but
only if it is recognized to be insufficient, depriving the
historic fact of its depth and putting the historic process
on a plane of only two dimensions.

But to inquire seriously into the reason why those

variations in the philosophic, political, or artistic manner of thinking come about means to set for oneself a question of enormous size. It is like asking why times change, why we neither think nor feel today as we did a hundred years ago, why humanity does not live still and quiet in the same unvaried repertory of thought and action, but wanders, always restless, unfaithful to itself, fleeing today from its own yesterdays, and with equal enthusiasm modifying the conduct of its heart and the shape of its hat. In short, why there is history.

I need not tell you that we will respectfully shy away from so exalted a question. But it is important to say that the historians have, up to the present, left intact and unexplored the most basic reason for these historic changes. The fact that one man, or several men, may invent a new idea or a new way of feeling does not bring about a change in the face of history or the tone of the times, any more than does the color of the Atlantic Ocean change because a painter of seascapes plunges into it a brush laden with vermilion. But if a great mass of men should adopt that idea and vibrate in accord with that way of feeling, then the whole area of history, the face of the times, will be tinged with the new color. But the great mass of men do not adopt a new idea or respond to a peculiar way of feeling simply because it is preached to them. That idea and that way of feeling must be existent within them, its shape determined, innate, and ready. Were it not for that basic, spontaneous predisposition in the mass of men, every preacher would find himself preaching in the desert.

Thus it is that historic changes assume the birth of a type of man more or less distinct from those who came before; that is, they assume a change in the generations. For some years I have been preaching to the historians that the concept of the generation is the most important one in the whole of history. A new generation of historians must have reached the world, for I see that this idea has caught hold, and, of all places, in Germany.[2]

In order that anything important may change in the world, there must be a change in the prevailing type of man—and of course, woman; throngs of children must appear wearing a character which is very different from that which is old and homogeneous. These throngs constitute a generation; a human variety in the strict sense in which naturalists use the term. Its members come into the world dowered with certain typical characteristics, certain dispositions and preferences which give them a common physiognomy that marks them off from the previous generation.

But this idea injects a sudden energy and a dramatic drive into the fact, as elemental as it is unexplored, that at every moment of history there exists not one generation but three: the young, the mature, the old. This means that every historical actuality, every "today" involves—strictly speaking—three different actualities, three different "todays." Or, to put it another way, the present is rich in three great vital dimensions which live in it together, linked to one another whether they like it or not, and, because they are different, essentially hostile to each other. For some of them, "today" means being twenty, for others it means forty, for still others it means sixty; and out of the fact that three such different ways of life must constitute the same "today,"

[2] Lorenz, Harmack, and Dilthey each said something about the idea of the generations; but the most serious attempt to deal with it, as I set it forth in some of my books, is recognized in Pinder's volume, *Das Problem der Generationem*, 2nd edition, 1928. [See Ortega's *The Modern Theme*, 1933, and *Man and Crisis*, 1958. Norton, N.Y. Translator's note]

there arises the dynamic drama, the conflict and the collision which make up the background of historical material and of all present-day living together. And in the light of this observation the error which is hidden in the apparent clarity of a date becomes manifest. The year 1929 looks to be a single fragment of time, but in 1929 there lived a boy, a mature man, and an old one; that number is tripled in three different meanings, and at the same time it includes all three; it is the unity of an historic time with three different ages in it.

All of us are contemporaries, we all live in the same time and the same atmosphere, but we play our part in forming them in a different time. Only the coevals coincide with one another; [3] contemporaries are not coevals. In history it is important to distinguish between the state of being coeval and that of being contemporary. Lodged together in a single external and chronological fragment of time are three different and vital times. This is what I usually call history's essential anachronism. It is thanks to that internal lack of equilibrium that history moves, changes, wheels and flows. If all contemporaries were coevals, history would stop as if paralyzed, petrified in one definitive gesture, lacking all chance of any radical innovation. I once pictured a generation as "A caravan within which man moves a prisoner, but at the same time, a voluntary one at heart, and content. He moves within it faithful to the poets of his age, to the political ideas of his time, to the type of woman triumphant in his youth, and even to the fashion of walking which he employed at twenty-five. From time to time he sees another caravan pass with a strange and curious

[3] In the volume cited, Pinder misses this distinction in my idea of the generations, although it is the crucial point. He was only able to read that part of my work which was translated into German.

profile; this is the other generation. Perhaps celebrations on a feast day may bring the two together, may blend them; but as the hour of normal living approaches the somewhat chaotic fusion divides into two organic groups. Each individual mysteriously recognizes all of the rest of his collectivity, as the ants in each of any hill recognize each other by a peculiar pattern of odor.

"The discovering that we are fatally inscribed within a certain group having its own age and style of life is one of the melancholy experiences which, sooner or later, befalls every sensitive man. A generation is an integrated manner of existence, or, if you prefer, a fashion in living, which fixes itself indelibly on the individual. Among certain savage peoples the members of each coeval group are recognized by their tattooing. The fashion in epidermal design which was in vogue when they were adolescents has remained encrusted in their beings." [4]

"This fate, like all fates, has soft spots through which certain individuals dowered with genius can escape. There are those who keep into their late years an inexhaustible flexibility and an enduring youthfulness which makes it possible for them to be reborn and remade two or three times in their life spans. Men of this kind have the character of precursors, and in them the new generation feels a sense of the elder brother who came ahead of his time. But they are the exceptions which, in the biological kingdom more than in any other, confirm the rule."

The problem which this need to feel oneself inscribed in a generation poses for every one of us can serve as an example of what I have called the art of life. One regards

[4] See *Man and Crisis*, pp. 44 ff. There is no indication as to the source of the following quoted paragraph. [Translator's note]

it as a doom, but the fact that some people escape it, in that they enjoy a longer youth, indicates that it is a fate full of holes, an elastic fatality, or, as the marvelous Bergson would say, *une fatalité modifiable*. When you feel in your heart that a reasonably characteristic phenomenon of our time is alien and undecipherable, it means that something inside of you wants to grow old. In every organism, individual or social, there is a tendency, amounting at times to a voluptuous desire, to let go of the present which is always innovation and to fall back out of sheer inertia into that which is past and habitual; a tendency to make itself gradually archaic.

When the man who has cultivated physical exercise reaches fifty, he tends to abandon such exercises and to take his ease. If he lets himself do this, he is lost. His muscles will lose their elasticity and become inevitably decrepit. But if, resisting the delights of repose, he avoids that first desire to abandon exercise and presses vigorously forward, he finds with some amazement that his muscles still possess an unexpectedly youthful reserve. This suggests that rather than abandoning ourselves to that fate which would imprison us within a generation we must work against it, and renew ourselves in the youthful fashion of the life which is crowding at our heels. Do not forget that infection is characteristic of every living thing. Illness is contagious, but so is health; vice and virtue are both catching, so are youth and old age. As you know, there is no chapter in modern biology so full of promise as the experimental study of rejuvenation. Within certain limits, and given a prescribed physical and moral hygiene, it is now quite possible to prolong one's youth without selling one's soul to the devil. He who ages early does it because he wants to, or better, because he does not want to go on living, because he is incapable of forcing himself to live vigorously. Not well rooted in his own destiny, a parasite on his own life, the flow of time drags him back into the past.

But when this prolongation of youth is no longer possible, one can still determine handsomely to be generous and, even though unable to live the new life that surges up, one can rejoice that others can live it, hope that the future will be different from our time, leave to that future its youth and its invading novelty. This is the problem of the mature man; the past pulls at him and sets up a resentment within him, a bitterness toward the future. He feels his youth still close beside him, but no longer in him; close at hand, but at the margin, like the trophy, the lance, and the mailed shirt which hang on the wall—war souvenirs grown feeble and paralytic. Now that one can no longer return to one's own youth, let another youth come!

In the Sahara there is a saying which, in its quiet phrase, paints an entire desert scene where men, flocks, and beasts of burden must crowd into one small oasis. It says, very simply, "Drink from the well, and yield your place to another." It is a symbol of the generations, as well as of the caravans.

This advice on an important matter of vital hygiene has led us far from the path we were traveling. I was trying to say that the linking together of three generations in a single present brings about the change in the times. The son's generation is always a bit different from his father's: it represents a new level from which to savor existence. Ordinarily the difference between sons and fathers is small, so that what predominates is the common nucleus in which they coincide, and the sons can see themselves as continuing and perfecting the type of life which their fathers led. But at times the distance between them is enormous; the new generation finds hardly any community of interest with the past. Then one speaks of a crisis in history.

Ours is such a time, and in a superlative degree. Although the change was being prepared subterraneously, it broke through the surface so suddenly, and with such speed, that within a few years it transformed the entire aspect of life. For many, many years I kept prophesying this imminent and total transformation. It was in vain. I reaped only censure; my prophecy was attributed to an itch for novelty. Not until events in all their crude reality arrived were the malicious tongues silenced. Yet here it is, all about us, a new life . . .

But no, it is not here yet. The change is going to be far more radical than what we are now seeing, and it will penetrate so far down through the various deep strata of human life that, taught by past experience, I am not disposed to tell you all that I foresee. It would be useless, it would frighten you without convincing you, and it would frighten for the reason that it would not be understood, or better, because it would be badly understood.

What we see now is an advance wave, just breaking, of the new time to come; whoever wishes to save himself must leap to ride it. He who resists, he who does not want to understand the new face which life is taking on, will be caught and submerged in the inevitable backwash of the past in every phase and meaning of life—in his work if he is an intellectual or an artist, in his love affairs if he is a romantic, in his political life if he is ambitious.

It is useful to have taken this first look at the theme of the generations. But what I have said is only a first contact, an external view of this tremendous and fundamental fact which we are going to meet in a much more vigorous and forceful fashion when the moment comes to examine what we call so gallantly and fearlessly— perhaps for the very reason that we do not quite know what we are saying—"our life."

But now let me try to point out the most immediate forces which, in the last sixty years of the nineteenth century, brought about the contracting, the narrowing of the philosophic mind, and, inversely, those which led to its present health and expanding vigor.

You will note that every science or branch of knowledge has its theme, the subject which that science knows about, or tries to know, and also that it has a special manner, a way of knowing what it knows. Mathematics, for example, has a subject—numbers and their extension— very different from the subject proper to biology, which is the phenomena of living organisms. But in addition, mathematics differs from biology in its manner of knowledge, in its kind of knowing. For the mathematician, to know is to be able to deduce a proposition by means of a system of rigorous reasoning which is ultimately founded on indubitable evidence. Biology, on the other hand, contents itself with generalizations which are approximated from the imprecise facts offered to us by the senses. As ways and kinds of knowledge, the two sciences are very different—the mathematical is exemplary, the biological is very rough and uncouth. On the other hand, mathematics has the inconvenience that the objects for which its theories are valid are not real, but are, as Descartes and Leibnitz said, "imaginary." But note also that in the sixteenth century there began an intellectual discipline—Galileo's *nuovo scienza*, which on the one hand has the deductive rigor of mathematics, and on the other speaks to us of real objects—of the stars, and, in general, of bodies. This is the first time in the long panorama of human thought that this happened; for the first time there came into existence a kind of knowledge which was obtained by means of precise deductions and at the same time was confirmed by sensory observation of the facts; that is to say, it tolerated a double criterion of certainty—pure reasoning, by which we believe we arrive at certain conclusions, and simple perception, which confirms the conclusions of pure theory. The unbreakable union of both criteria constitutes the manner of knowing called experimental which characterizes physics.

It is in no way strange that a science dowered with such fortunate conditions should from that point on begin to stand out above the others, and to attract the attention of the best minds. Even from an exclusively theoretic point of view, even as mere theory, or knowledge in the strictest sense, there is no doubt that physics is an intellectual marvel. At the same time, it was concealed from no one that the coincidence between the deductive conclusions of reasoned physics and the sensory observations of experiment was not quite exact, but only approximated. It is also true that this approximation was so great that it did not impede the practical march of the science.

Nevertheless, it is certain that those two characteristics of physics—its practical exactitude and its confirmation by perceptible facts (do not forget the pathetic circumstance that the stars themselves seem to submit to laws which the astronomers lay down for them, and with a rare fidelity meet the appointment made for them at this hour and at that place in the enormous firmament)—those two characteristics, as I say, would not have been enough to carry the science of physics to the extraordinary triumph which it then achieved. A third peculiarity appeared which enormously enhanced this manner of knowing. It happened that the truths of physics, over and above its theoretic qualities, were highly useful to man's practical necessities. By making use of them, man could intervene in nature and bend it to his own advantage.

This third characteristic, its practical utility for man's dominion over matter, is not exactly a virtue or a test of the perfection of physics as a theory and a form of knowledge. In Greece, this utilitarian fruitfulness would not have won a decisive influence over every mind, but in Europe it coincided with the predominance of a type of man—the so-called bourgeois—who felt no vocation for the contemplative or the theoretic, but only for the practical. The bourgeois wanted to settle himself comfortably in the world, and for his comfort to intervene in it, to modify it for his own pleasure. Therefore the bourgeois age is honored most of all for the triumph of industrialization, and in general, for those techniques which are useful to life—medicine, economics, administration. Physics acquired a peerless prestige because out of it came both medicine and the machine. The masses of the middle class became interested in it not out of intellectual curiosity, but through their material interests. It was in such an atmosphere that what we might call the "imperialism of physics" was produced.

Born and educated as we are in an age which shares this mode of feeling, it seems to us a very natural thing that first place among the various kinds of knowledge should be granted to that which, whatever its standing in theory, gives us domination over matter. But a new cycle is beginning within us; for no sooner do we see that this form of supremacy makes practical utility appear to be a norm of truth than we cease to be content. We begin to realize that this skill in dominating matter and making it conform to our wishes, this enthusiasm for comfort is, if one makes of it a principle, as open to argument as any other. Alerted by this suspicion, we begin to see that comfort is merely a subjective predilection, or to put it bluntly, a capricious desire which Western peoples have exercised for two hundred years, but which does not in itself reveal any superiority of character.

There are those who prefer the comfortable above all else, there are others who give it no major importance. While Plato was absorbed in formulating those thoughts which have made modern physics possible, and with it comfort, he led, like all the Greeks, a life which was very hard; insofar as modes of transportation, heating, and domestic arrangements were concerned, that life was actually barbarous. At the same moment of time the Chinese, who had never entertained a single scientific thought, never spun a theory, were weaving delightful fabrics, fabricating useful objects, and constructing items of exquisite comfort. While Plato's academy in Athens was inventing pure mathematics, men in Peking were inventing the pocket handkerchief.

Note, then, that the urge for the comfortable and the convenient which is the ultimate reason for a preference for physics is in no way an index of superiority. Certain periods have yielded to it, others have not. Everyone who is able to examine our own period with some degree of penetration believes that he foresees in the future an enthusiasm for comfort and convenience as an imperative of life and living which will be no more than lukewarm. Man then will make use of this facility, take care of it, conserve what of it has been achieved, and seek to increase it, but without enthusiasm and not for itself, but in order to be able to avoid exercises which are by no means comfortable.

It would be very interesting for a curious research scholar to start with the fact that the urge for comfort, while not by itself a sign of progress, does appear in history scattered as if by chance among periods at very different levels: he would then search for the points of coincidence among these periods. Or to put it another way, he would be seeking to find what human condition it is that carries with it this devotion to the comfortable and the convenient.

I do not know what the results of such an inquiry might be. In passing, however, I would like to underline this coincidence; the two periods and places in history which have paid the greatest attention to comfort have been these last two European centuries and the great age of Chinese civilization. Between those two human worlds which are otherwise so disparate and different, what was there in common that produced this likeness? So far as I know, only this: during that European era the "good bourgeois" was in power, the type of man who represents the will and aims of the prosaic side of life; as for the Chinese, he is notoriously a born Philistine. (I say this casually, without formal charges or any insistence.) [5]

Here is the way in which the philosopher of the bourgeois, Auguste Comte, states the meaning of knowledge in his famous formula: "Science, d'où prévoyance; prévoyance, d'où action." That is, the reason for knowing is to be able to predict, and the reason for prediction

[5] Concerning the Philistine character of the Chinese, read what Count Keyserling has to say in his *Travel Diary of a Philosopher*.

is to make action possible. The result is that action—advantageous action, of course—becomes the thing that defines the truth of knowledge. At the end of the past century a great physicist, Boltzmann, said, "In the last analysis, neither logic nor philosophy nor metaphysics decides whether a thing is true or false; action alone is decisive. For this reason I do not consider the victories of technique as simple secondary precipitates of natural science, but as logical proofs of that science. If we had not proposed those practical conquests we would not know how we ought to reason. There are no correct reasonings except those which have practical results." [6] In his *Discours sur l'esprit positif* that same Comte had already suggested that it is technique which regiments science, and not the opposite. According to this way of thinking, utility is therefore not an unforeseen precipitate, a *pourboire* for the truth, as it were, but the reverse; truth is the intellectual precipitate of practical utility. A little later, in the infant dawning of our century, a philosophy was made out of this idea which is called pragmatism. With that amiable cynicism which is characteristic of the Yankees, characteristic of every new people (a new people, just arrived, seems always to be an *enfant terrible*), pragmatism in North America dared to proclaim this thesis—"There is no other truth than success in dealing with things." And with this thesis, as audacious as it is ingenuous, and so ingenuously audacious, the Northern lobe of the American continent made its entrance into the age-old history of philosophy. [7]

Do not confuse the small esteem which pragmatism

---

[6] See Scheler, *Forms of Knowing and of Society*.
[7] With this I suggest that in pragmatism, and especially in its audacity and ingenuity there is something profoundly true, even though it be centrifugal.

merits, as a philosophy and a general thesis of life, with any preconceived, arbitrary and bigoted disdain toward the fact of human practicality as contrasted with pure contemplation, and favoring the latter. Here we are trying to twist the neck of all bigotries, including that scientific and cultural bigotry which went into ecstasies over pure knowledge without making a dramatic question out of it. This divides us radically from the ancient thinkers—from Plato as from Aristotle—and becomes one of the most serious themes for our meditation. When we plunge down into the decisive problem, which is the defining of "our life," we will try very hard to define and delimit the anatomy of that perennial duality which divides life into *vita contemplativa* and *vita activa*, into action and contemplation, into Martha and Mary.

At the moment we are only trying to suggest that the imperial triumph which physics enjoys is due not so much to its quality as a form of knowledge as to a social fact. Society became interested in physics because of its fruitful utility; over the course of a century this social interest has swelled to the point of hypertrophy the faith which physics has in itself. The same thing has happened to it that has happened to many a doctor. No one would consider medicine as a model among sciences; nevertheless, the worship which is lavished on the doctor in the homes of the aged (as in other days it was lavished on the magician) gives him a security in his post and his person, an impertinent audacity which is as amusing as it is lacking in reason; for while the doctor makes use of the results of science he is not usually a man of science or a theoretician.

Good fortune, favor on the part of the social atmosphere about us, is likely to lift us above ourselves, to make us petulant and aggressive. This happened to the physicists; and therefore the intellectual life of Europe has for almost a hundred years suffered from what one might call the "terrorism of the laboratories."

Overwhelmed by this superiority, the philosopher was ashamed of being overwhelmed, which meant that he became ashamed of not being a physicist. As the problems which are genuinely philosophic do not permit of solution according to the method of the physical sciences, the philosopher gave up any attempt to attack them; he renounced his philosophy, contracting it to a minimum, putting it humbly at the service of the physics. He decided that the only philosophic theme worth pursuing was meditation on the fact of physics, that philosophy was merely a theory of knowledge, and nothing more.

Kant was the first to adopt such an attitude in a radical form; he did not interest himself directly in the great cosmic problems, but with the imperative hand of a town policeman he stopped all philosophic traffic— twenty-six centuries of metaphysical thought—by saying, "Let all philosophizing remain suspended until this question is answered: How are synthetic judgments possible *a priori?*" Well, now, "synthetic judgments *a priori*" meant to him physics, the *factum* of the physio-mathematical science.

But these statements of the problem as he saw it were not even a theory of knowledge. Their point of departure was the knowledge of physics as it existed, and they did not ask "What is knowledge?"

3

The "Theme of Our Times." Science as Mere Symbolism. The Sciences in Rebellion. Why Is Philosophy? Exactness in Science and in Philosophic Knowledge. Postscript.

I HAVE been leading you just across the threshold of what I meant to develop during the previous discussion. I wanted to state the immediate reasons, insufficient though they may be, why the mind of the philosopher was for a century narrowing and contracting, and why, on the other hand, it is now beginning to expand. I had only time enough to talk about the first point, telling you that philosophy had stayed prone, humiliated by the imperialism of physics and frightened by the terrorism of the laboratories. The natural sciences dominated the surrounding atmosphere, and atmosphere is one of the ingredients of our personality just as atmospheric pressure is one of the factors which order and compose our physical shape. If it did not press close about us and set limits for us we would, as Horace wished, touch the stars with our heads; that is to say, we would be formless, indefinite, and impersonal. Each one of us is half

what he is and half what he is made to be by the atmosphere in which he lives. When the latter coincides favor-
ably with the peculiar make-up of the individual, our
personality becomes entirely realized, feels itself supported and confirmed by its surroundings and is spurred
to an expansion of its interior resources. When the surrounding atmosphere (which is a part of us) is hostile to
us, it forces us tó a perpetual state of struggle and dis-
sociation, it depresses us and makes it difficult for our
personality to develop and to come to full fruition. This
latter is what happened to philosophers in the atmosphere
imposed upon them by the tyrants of the experiment.

I need not tell you that none of my words, however
sharp they may sound, are meant as censure, either moral
or intellectual, of those men of science or those philosophers whom I have been discussing. They were as they
had to be, and it has been extraordinarily fruitful for the
world that they were. Several qualities of the new philosophy owe their being to that period of forced humility,
as the Hebrew soul was rendered more subtle and interesting after its slavery in Babylon. We are already
seeing in concrete terms how the philosophers, having
suffered the disdain of those men of science who kept
throwing up at them the charge that philosophy is not a
science, now find pleasure in this insult—at least it pleases
me; catching it in mid-air, we toss it back, saying "Philosophy is not a science, because it is much more than a
science."

But now we must ask ourselves what has produced
this new enthusiasm of philosophers for their philosophy,
this confidence in the meaning of their work, and this
resolute air which moves us to be philosophers without
fear or favor, to be philosophers shamelessly, auda-
ciously, even a bit gaily.

In my judgment, two great events have favored this change.

We have seen that philosophy had been reduced to little more than a theory of knowledge. This is what the greater part of the books on philosophy which were published between 1860 and 1920 call themselves. And I also noted the extremely surprising fact that in the books thus entitled one would never find seriously posed the question, "What is knowledge?" This is a rather monstrous omission; apparently we have stumbled on one of those cases of determined blindness which the pressure of the atmosphere about him produces in man, imposing on him as evident and indisputable precisely those assumptions which it would be most useful to discuss. These instances of blindness vary from one period to another, but they are never absent, and we have our own kinds today. The reason for this will occupy us later, when we see that the process of living always grows *out of* or *is based on* certain assumptions; these are like the soil on which we stand, or which we use as a point of departure.

And this is true in every field, in science as in politics, in morals, in art. Every idea is thought, every picture painted, out of certain assumptions or conventions which are so basic, so firmly fixed for the one who thought the idea or who painted the picture that he neither pays heed to them, nor, for that matter, introduces them into his picture or his idea; nor do we find them there in any guise except as *pre*-supposed and left, as it were, at one side. This is why we sometimes fail to understand an idea or a picture; we lack the clue to the enigma, the key to the secret convention.

And let me repeat that as each era, or more precisely each generation, takes as its point of departure a set of

assumptions which are more or less different from those
that went before or will come after, this means that the
prevailing system of truths and values—esthetic, moral,
political, or religious—has an inexorable dimension in
terms of history; these are related to a certain vital
human chronology, they have value for certain men, and
nothing more. Truth is historical. How truth can, and
indeed must, claim nevertheless to be super-historical—
not relative but absolute—is the great question. Many of
you know that for me, the resolving of this question
within the realm of the possible is the theme of our
time.[1]

The assumption, neither discussed nor discussable,
which the thinker of the mid-nineteenth century carried
in his very bloodstream, was that in the strict sense of
the term there is no other knowledge of the world than
that contained in physical science, that there is no other
truth about reality than "physical truth." Earlier, we
saw dimly that perhaps other types of "truth" might
exist, and that "physical truth," even when seen at a
distance, certainly has two qualities that are admirable;
its exactness, and the fact that it is governed by a double
criterion of certitude, rational deduction on the one
hand, and on the other, confirmation by the senses. But
these qualities, magnificent though they be, are not
enough to ensure that there is no more perfect form of
knowledge in the world, no higher type of truth than
physical truth and the science of physics. In order to
affirm this, one would have to develop completely the
question, "What would be the form of knowledge that
we might consider exemplary, the prototype of truth, if
we held strictly to the meaning which the verb *to know*
carries within itself?" Only when we know what knowl-

[1] See *The Modern Theme*. [Translator's note]

edge is, in the fullest meaning of the term, can we see whether or not those forms, those fragments of knowledge which man possesses, fulfill this meaning or merely approximate it. Until this is done, one cannot talk seriously of a theory of knowledge; as philosophy in these last years has pretended to be nothing more than that, the result is that it has not been even that.

But meanwhile physics was growing, and since 1880 has been reaching such a breadth and perfection, such a degree of precision, within a sphere of observations so gigantic, that it found itself needing to reform its principles. Let this be said for the sake of anyone who holds the popular belief that the modification of a doctrinal system suggests that a science has very little firmness. The truth is just the opposite. It was for the very reason that the principles of Galileo and Newton were valid that the portentous development of physics was possible; this development reached a limit which made it necessary to broaden those principles, and in the process to purify them. This brought the "crisis in principles," the *Grundlagekrise* from which physics suffers today, and which is a most fortunate illness of growth. I do not know why we so often assume that the word "crisis" has a connotation of sadness; a crisis is no more than a deep and intense change; it may be a change for the worse, but it can also be a change for the better, which is what is happening with the present crisis in physics.

There is no better sign of maturity in a science than a crisis in principles. It assumes that the science finds itself so sure of itself that it can afford the luxury of submitting its principles boldly to revision, which means that it demands of them a still greater vigor and firmness. The intellectual vigor of a man, like that of a science, is measured by the dose of skepticism and doubt which he is capable of digesting and assimilating. The sturdy theory, far from being an ingenuous confidence which has never known vacillation, is nourished on doubt; it is by no means an innocent trust, but a sureness in the midst of storm, a confidence amid lack of confidence. Certainly it is confidence, triumphing over lack of confidence, which gives a measure of the intellectual vigor that prevails. On the other hand, doubt which is not subdued, lack of confidence which is not digested and assimilated becomes—neurasthenia.

The principles of physics are the ground beneath this science; on them the investigator moves. But when there is need to reform them, they must be reformed not from within, but from without. In order to remake the soil one must, of course, be able to stand on the subsoil. Hence the physicists see themselves obliged to philosophize about their science, and in this field the most characteristic thing happening at the moment is the philosophic preoccupation of the physicists. From Poincaré, Mach, and Duhem to Einstein and Weyl, with their disciples and followers, the physicists themselves have been building a theory of physical knowledge. To be sure, they have at hand all the great influences of the philosophic past, but the curious part of the matter is that while philosophy itself exaggerated the cult of physics as a type of knowledge, the physicists' theory ends by the discovery that physics is an inferior form of knowledge, that it is, in point of fact, a symbolic knowledge.

The manager of the Kursaal who counts the coat hangers used in the coatroom thus finds out how many coats and wraps hung from those hangers, and thanks to this, he knows approximately the number of people who attended the performance. Yet he has seen neither the garments nor the people.

If one compares the content of physics with the physical world one finds very little similarity between them. They are like two different languages which can only be translated into one another. Physics has no more than a symbolic correspondence with the world about us.

How do we know that physics is this thing? Because many other correspondences are equally possible; as for instance, the ordering of things in the most diverse forms.

On a certain solemn occasion [2] Einstein summed up the position of physics insofar as knowledge is concerned, with these words: "The evolution of our science has shown that among the imaginable theoretic constructions there is, in every case, always one which shows a decided superiority over the others. No one who has gone deeply into the matter will deny that the world of our perceptions determines practically and without ambiguity which theoretic system must be chosen. *Nevertheless*, there is no logical road which leads to the principles of theory."

That is to say, many theories are equally adequate and the superiority of any single one is, strictly speaking, founded solely on practical reasons. The facts recommend it, but they do not impose it.

Only at certain points does the body of doctrine which belongs to physics touch the reality of nature: these points are the experiments. The body of doctrine could always be shifted as long as the points remain in contact. The experiment is a manipulation by which we intervene in nature and force it to respond to us. The experiment is not a matter of nature *qua* nature revealing herself to us in her own way, but only her specific re-

[2] His speech to Max Planck on Planck's sixtieth birthday.

action in the face of our specific intervention. Consequently—and this I want to emphasize in a formal statement—the so-called physical reality is a dependent reality and not an absolute one; it is reality, a quasi-reality—because it is conditional and relative to man. In short, what physics calls reality is what happens if it executes a manipulation. Only in the operation of the latter does that reality exist.

Philosophy, on the other hand, searches out as reality that which is completely independent of any actions of ours, that which specifically does not depend on such actions; indeed, the actions depend on the fullness of the reality which is sought.

It was shameful that, after the philosophers had erected such extensive theories of knowledge, the physicists should have had to shoulder the task of giving final precision to the character of their knowledge, and to show us that far from representing an exemplary prototype of knowing, physics is, strictly speaking, an inferior kind of theory, very far from the object which it seeks to penetrate.

Hence these sciences—and most of all physics—advance by making out of their limitations the creative principles of their concepts. In order to improve they do not try to take a utopian leap over and beyond their own shadow or to surpass their own fateful limit; on the contrary, they accept this latter with pleasure, and holding it close, installing themselves inside it with no regrets, they succeed in reaching plenitude. The opposite attitude prevailed during the last century. Each one then aspired to a life which had no limitations, each aimed to be what the others were and he was not. It was the century in which one form of music, Wagner's music, was not content with being music but aspired to be a substitute for philosophy and even for religion; it was the century in which physics desired to be metaphysics and philosophy wished to be physics, when poetry wanted to take the place of painting and melody; politics was not content with being politics, but aspired to be a religious creed, and what is more absurd, to make men happy.

In the new attitude of those sciences which prefer to withdraw each into its own corner, its own orbit, is there not the mark of a new human sensitiveness which tries to resolve the problem of life by a method the reverse of that which prevailed earlier? A method in which each being and each occupation accepts its own destiny, drives deep into it, and rather than indulging in the illusion of moving elsewhere, fills its own authentic and untransferable outline to the very edges? I drop that suggestion here in passing, and we will come to it another day.

Nevertheless, this recent *capitis diminutio* of physics as theory, acting on the spiritual state of philosophies, has had the effect of freeing them for their own vocation. Idolatrous worship of the experiment having been overcome, and physical knowledge having retreated within its own modest orbit, the mind remains free and open for other ways of knowing, and sensibilities are again alert to those problems which are truly philosophic.

This deprives physics of none of its glory; on the contrary, it emphasizes its prodigious solidity and its present fertility. Conscious of its power as a science, physics disdains any fraudulent claims of mystical superiorities. It knows that it is no more than a symbolic form of knowledge, and that is enough; being only this, it is today one of the most formidable and dramatic things that are happening in the world. If it were true that Europe is truly cultured—an assumption which is far from true—the crowds would gather day by day in front of newspaper offices to follow the state of physical investigations. For the situation is one of such fruitfulness, new and fabulous discoveries are so close, that there is not the slightest exaggeration in predicting a sudden entry into a new cosmic landscape, into a concept of the physical world which will be profoundly different from that which has sheltered us up to now. And that situation is of such imminence that I could not say, nor could the famous physicists who listen to me, whether at this very moment the colossal new idea may not have sprung into being in some head in Germany or England.[3]

Now we see that what held us on our knees before the so-called "scientific truth," that is, the type of truth proper to physics and its related disciplines, was a superstition.

You will remember that the situation which was previously described could be formulated as follows: each science accepts its own limitation and out of it makes its positive method. The fact which I am about to sketch for you represents a further step in that same sense: each science makes itself independent of the rest, that is to say, it will not accept their jurisdiction.

Here, too, the new physics offers us the best and most famous example. For Galileo, the mission of physics was to discover the special laws which rule over bodies, "over and above general geometric laws." That these latter ruled in physical phenomena he never for a moment doubted. Therefore he spent no time in arranging experiments which should demonstrate nature's docility to Euclidean theories. He accepted the superior authority

[3] Written before nuclear fission. [Translator's note]

of geometry over physics as a thing which was self-evident and inescapable, or to put it another way, he believed that geometric laws were physical laws *ex abundantia*, and in high degree. In Einstein's work the point of greatest genius lies in the decision with which he freed himself from this traditional prejudice; when he observes that phenomena are not behaving according to Euclid's law and finds himself in the midst of the conflict between the jurisdiction of geometry and that which belongs exclusively to physics, he does not hesitate to declare the latter sovereign. Comparing his solution with that of Lorentz one notes two mental types which are utterly opposed to one another. In order to explain Michelson's experiment Lorentz, following in the footsteps of tradition, resolved that physics would adapt itself to geometry. A body must contract so that geometric space may continue sovereign and intact. Einstein, on the contrary, decided that geometry and space would adapt themselves to physics and the phenomena of bodies.

We so frequently find parallel attitudes in the other sciences that I am surprised not to have seen this characteristic of recent thought, general and prominent as it is, noted elsewhere.

Pavlov's theory of reflexes and Hering's theory of the effect of light on man are two attempts, classic at this time, to construct a physiology which shall be independent both of physics and psychology. In them the biological phenomenon is taken as such insofar as those elements are concerned that are alien to the common condition of physical or psychological fact, and it is treated by methods of investigation which are exclusive to physiology.

But the place where this new scientific temperament

appears most sharply, almost to the point of public
scandal, is in mathematics. The subjection of mathematics to logic had in recent generations reached such a
point as to make them almost identical. But then the
Dutchman Brouwer discovered that the axiom of logic
which is called the "excluded middle" had no value for
mathematical entities and that it was necessary to create
a mathematics "without logic," faithful only to itself,
not docile to alien axioms.

Once we have observed this tendency in the new
thinking, it cannot surprise us that a theology has appeared which rebels against the authority of philosophy.
Until recently, theology showed an eagerness to adapt
revealed truth to philosophic reason, an attempt to make
the unreason of the mystery admissible to such reason.
But the new "dialectic theology" breaks sharply with
such musty usage and declares the knowing of God to be
independent and "totally" sovereign. Thus it inverts the
attitude of the theologian, whose specific task used to
consist in taking revealed truth from man and his
scientific norms, therefore in talking about God from the
point of view of man. This produced a theology which
was anthropocentric. But Barth and his colleagues re-
versed this process and elaborated a theology which is
theocentric.

Out of himself and his intrahuman mind, man can by
definition know nothing of God. He is merely the re-
ceiver of the knowledge which God has of Himself, and
which He sends to man, bit by bit, by means of revelation. The theologian has no other duty than to make
pure the ear into which God breathes his own truth, a
divine truth which cannot be measured against any
human truth, and which by the same token is independent. In this form theology cuts itself loose from the

jurisdiction of philosophy. The shift is the more notable in that it was produced within Protestantism, where the humanization of theology and its surrender to philosophy had advanced much further than in the Catholic field.

The sciences are now dominated by a trend which is diametrically opposed to that obtaining toward the end of the nineteenth century. At that time one science or another tried to rule the rest, to extend its own domestic method over them, and the rest humbly tolerated this invasion. Now each science not only accepts its native defects but repels every pretense that another can make laws for it.

Similar phenomena exist in modern art and politics.

These are the most important characteristics of the intellectual mode which has shown itself in these past years. I believe they can usher in a great period of human thought; but with one reservation. The sciences cannot remain in this position of unruly independence. Without losing what they have now won, they must somehow achieve articulation one with another, without any one of them holding another in subjection. This can be done only by basing themselves anew on philosophy. The growing frequency with which the individual scientist feels himself forced—by the very urgency of his own problems—to dive into philosophic waters is a clear indication that scientists are moving toward this new procedure.

But my subject now does not leave me free to go off into a consideration of the future of science; what I have sketched concerning its present is only meant to show the prevailing conditions in the intellectual atmosphere which favored a return to a philosophy in the great tradition, thus counteracting the shrinking tendencies of the past hundred years. In the currents of public opinion which now surround us the philosopher himself finds new courage to make himself at once independent and faithful to the limitations of his own destiny.

But there is another and stronger reason why the time may be ripe for a rebirth of philosophy. The tendency on the part of each science to accept its own limitations and to proclaim itself independent creates only a set of negative conditions insufficient to overcome the obstructions which have paralyzed the philosophic calling for a hundred years: they do not nourish that vocation nor do they spur it on to greater energy.

Why, then, is man returning to philosophy? Why is philosophy again becoming a normal vocation? Obviously one goes back to a thing for the same essential reason that took him to it in the first place. If not, the return lacks sincerity, becomes a false and pretended return.

This leads us to ask why it occurred to man to create philosophy in the first place. What made man—yesterday, today, or any other day—begin to philosophize? It is important to bring this thing which we call philosophy clearly to mind so that we can answer the "why?" of its use.

From this new point of view, our form of knowledge shows all the characteristics it had in former periods, but shaped by the progress of thinking into a new and more rigorous form. What does this resurgent philosophy look like to our own eyes?

I am going to answer this question with a series of sketches in the shape of formulae which gradually, over the course of this discussion, will reveal their meaning.

One might begin by defining philosophy as knowledge

of the Universe. But this definition, while accurate enough, allows the very thing that is specific to escape from us, namely the peculiar dramatic quality and the tone of intellectual heroism peculiar to philosophy and only philosophy. In effect, that definition seems to balance the one we were giving for physics when we said that it is knowledge of matter. But the fact is that the philosopher does not set himself in front of his object—the Universe—as does the physicist in front of his object, which is matter. The physicist begins by defining the profile, the outline of matter, and only then does he start working in an attempt to understand its internal structure. The mathematician defines number and extension by a similar process. Thus all the individual sciences begin by marking off for themselves a bit of the Universe, by limiting their problem, which, once limited, ceases in part to be a problem. Or to put it another way, the physicist and the mathematician know in advance the extent of their object and its essential attributes; therefore they begin not with the problem, but with something which they give or take as already known.

But the Universe on whose investigation the philosopher sets out, audacious as an Argonaut—no one knows what this is. *Universe* is an enormous and monolithic word which, like a vague and vast gesture, conceals this concept—everything that is—rather than stating it. Everything that is—for the moment, that is the Universe. That, note it well, nothing more than that, for when we think the concept, "everything there is," we do not know what that "everything there is" may be; the only thing we think is a negative concept, namely the negation of that which would only be a part, a piece, a fragment. *So the philosopher, in contradistinction to every other scientist, sets sail for the unknown as such.* The more or less known is a part, a portion, a splinter of the Universe. The philosopher sets himself in front of his object in an attitude which is different from that of any other expert; the philosopher does not know what his object is, of it he knows only this—first, that it is no one of the other objects; second, that it is an integral object, the authentic whole, that which leaves nothing outside, and by the same token, the only one which is sufficient unto itself. No other one of the objects which are known or suspected possesses this condition. Therefore the Universe is that which basically we do not know, that of which we are absolutely ignorant insofar as its positive content is concerned.

Swinging around this subject on an earlier spiral, we could say that to the other sciences their object is given, but the object of philosophy is precisely that which cannot be given; because it is the whole, and because it is not given, it must in a very special sense be that which is sought for, perennially sought for. There is nothing strange in the fact that the very science whose object must at the start be sought for, the science that is problematical even as to its object and its subject matter, should have a life less tranquil than the others, and should not at first sight enjoy what Kant called *der sichere Gang*. Philosophy, which is pure theoretic heroism, will never have this sure, peaceful and bourgeois stage. Like its object, philosophy will consist in being the universal and absolute science which is sought for. Thus Aristotle, the first master of our discipline, calls it philosophy, the science which is sought for—ζητουμένη ἐπιστήμη.

Not even in the aforesaid definition—philosophy is knowledge of the Universe—does knowledge mean the same as in the individual sciences. In the strict and primary sense of the word, knowledge means a positive and concrete solution to a problem, that is, a perfect penetration of the object by the mind of its subject. Yet if knowledge were only that, philosophy could not bind itself to be that. Imagine that our philosophy should come to demonstrate that the ultimate reality of the Universe is made up of a being which is completely capricious, of a will which is unpredictable and irrational —in effect, this is what Schopenhauer believed he had discovered. Then there would be no possibility of total penetration of the object by the subject—to intelligence that irrational reality would be opaque—yet it cannot be doubted that this would be a perfect philosophy, no less perfect than others in which the being is wholly transparent to thought and docile to reason, which is the basic idea of all rationalism.

So we must protect the meaning of the word *knowledge*, and note that if in effect it does mean primarily that full entrance into thinking about the Universe, there will be a scale of values for knowledge, depending on how close it comes to that ideal. Philosophy must begin by defining that maximum concept and at the same time must leave itself open to those lesser grades which in the last analysis will be another set of ways of knowing. For this reason, when I define philosophy as knowledge of the Universe I propose that we understand an integral system of intellectual attitudes in which the desire for absolute knowledge is organized methodically. In order that a complex of thoughts may be a philosophy, the decisive thing is that the reaction of the intellect to the Universe shall also be universal, integral—in short, that it be a system which is absolute.

Thus one of the obligations of philosophy is to take a theoretic position, to confront every problem—not meaning thereby to solve it, but to demonstrate positively that it cannot be solved. This is the characteristic of philosophy as compared with the sciences. When these latter meet a problem which for them is insoluble they simply cease to deal with it. Philosophy, on the other hand, admits from the start that the world may be a problem which in itself is insoluble. And to demonstrate this fully would be the task of a philosophy which would completely fulfill its position as such.

For the uses of pragmatism, and everything that is called science, a problem which is insoluble is not a problem—and by "insoluble" they mean, not to be solved by methods which have been previously recognized. To them a problem is "that which can be solved," and as the solution consists in certain manipulations, the definition comes to include "that which can be done." Pragmatism is, in effect, the practice that supplants all theory. (Remember Peirce's definition of pragmatism.) But at the same time it is the sincere theory in which the cognitive manner of certain sciences is expressed, the way of knowing possessed by those individual sciences which conserve a vestige of that practical attitude which is not a pure zeal for knowing, and, by the same token, is an acceptance of a problem without limits.

Where, one asks, does this appetite for the Universe, for the wholeness of the world, which is the root of philosophy, come from? To put it simply, that appetite, seeming peculiar to philosophy, is in fact the native and spontaneous attitude of the live mind. In the very act of living we sense, clearly or cloudily, a world about us which we assume to be complete. It is the man of science, the mathematician, the scientist, who cuts down through that integral aspect of our living world, who isolates a piece of it and out of this makes his own particular question. If knowledge of the Universe, if philosophy, does not yield truths of the same type as "scientific truth," so much the worse for scientific truth.

"Scientific truth is characterized by its exactness and the rigorous quality of its assumptions. But experimental science wins these admirable qualities at the cost of maintaining itself on a plane of secondary problems and leaving the decisive and ultimate questions intact. Out of this renunciation it makes its essential virtue, and for this, if for nothing else, it deserves applause. But experimental science is only a meager portion of the mind and the organism. Where it stops, man does not stop. If the physicist stays the hand with which he delineates things at the point where his methods end, the human being who stands behind every physicist prolongs the line and carries it on to the end, just as our eye, seeing a portion of a broken arch, automatically completes the missing airy curve.

"The mission of physics is to find out from each existent fact just what its beginning was; that is, what was the preceding fact that caused it. But that beginning had in turn an earlier beginning, and thus on back to a first originating principle.

"The physicist renounces the search for this first principle of the Universe; in so doing he does well. But I repeat that the man in whom each physicist is lodged does not give up the search. With his consent or against his will, his soul is drawn toward that first and enigmatic cause. This is natural. To live is certainly to deal with the world, to turn toward it, to act within it, to be occupied with it. Hence, it is literally impossible for man, bound as he is by psychological necessity, to renounce the attempt to possess a complete idea of the world, an integral idea of the Universe. Be it crude or refined, with

our consent or without it, that transscientific picture of
the world is embodied in every spirit; it comes to govern
our existence much more effectively than does scientific
truth.

"The past century tried very hard to rein in the human
mind and hold it in check within the limits set by exactness. This violence, this turning the back on ultimate
problems was called 'agnosticism.' Such an effort is
neither justified nor plausible. That experimental science
may be incapable of resolving those fundamental questions in its own way is no reason why it should behave
like the fox with the high-hung grapes, should call them
'myths' and invite us to abandon them. How can we
live deaf to the last, dramatic questions? Where does the
world come from, whither is it going? What is the definitive power in the cosmos? What is the essential meaning
of life? Confined to a zone of intermediate and secondary
themes, we cannot breathe. We need a complete perspective, with foreground and background, not a maimed
and partial landscape, not a horizon from which the lure
of the great distances has been cut away. Lacking a set
of cardinal points, our footsteps would lack direction.
To assert that no manner of resolving the ultimate questions has yet been discovered is no valid excuse for a
lack of sensitiveness toward them. All the more reason
for feeling in the depths of our being their pressure and
their hurt! Whose hunger has ever been stilled by knowing that he will not be able to eat? Insoluble though they
be, those questions will continue to rise, pathetic, on the
clouded vault of the night, blinking at us like the twinkle
of a star. As Heine put it, the stars are the night's
thoughts, restless and golden. North and South help to
orient us despite their not being accessible cities reached
simply by buying a railroad ticket.

"What I mean by this is that we are given no escape from the ultimate questions. Whether we like it or not, they live, in one fashion or another, within us. 'Scientific truth' is exact, but it is incomplete and penultimate; it is of necessity embedded in another kind of truth, complete and ultimate, although inexact, which could be called 'myth.' Scientific truth floats, then, in mythology, and science itself, as a whole, is a myth, the admirable European myth." [4]

Postscript: The Origin of Knowledge

But if we ask whence comes that hunger for the Universe, for the whole mass of the world, which is the root of philosophy, Aristotle leaves us caught on a paling. To him the question is very simple, and he begins his *Metaphysics* by saying, "Man by nature feels the urge to know." To know is to be not content with things as presented to us, but to seek beyond their appearance for their being. This "being" of things is a strange condition: it is not made clear in things, but on the contrary, it throbs hidden within them, beneath them, beyond them. To Aristotle it seems "natural" that we should question that "beyond," when in fact the natural thing would be for us, who live our lives surrounded with things, to be content with them as they are. We have not the slightest information about their "being." It is things that are given us, not the being of things. There is in them no positive sign that they have a "being" behind them. Obviously the "beyond" of things is in no way within

[4] Ortega, "The Sportive Origin of the State," in *Toward a Philosophy of History*, Norton, 1941, a new edition of which will be published in 1961 under the title, *History as a System and Other Essays*. [Translator's note]

them.

It is said that man is naturally curious. And this is what Aristotle thinks when, asked "Why does man exert himself to know?" he answers, like one of Molière's doctors, "Because it is natural." "His eagerness to perceive, to look, is a sign that this urge to know is natural," he goes on. Here Aristotle recalls Plato, who classed both scientists and philosophers as *philotheamones*, "friends of looking," those who go to spectacles. But looking is the opposite of knowing: to look is to run the eyes over what is here, and knowing is to search for what is not here: the being of things. It is a refusal to be content with what can be seen, a denying that what can be seen is enough, a demand for the invisible, the "beyond."

With this and many other indications which abound in his books, Aristotle reveals his idea of the origin of knowledge. This would consist simply in the use of a faculty that man has, just as looking would be no more than using the power of sight. We have senses, we have a memory which preserves the data they gather, we have experience in which that memory makes its selections and decants the result. All these are native mechanisms of the human organism which man, like it or not, exercises. But none of this is knowledge. Not even though we add the other faculties more properly called "intellectual"—abstracting, collecting, comparing, and so on. Intelligence, or the combination of all those powers, is also a mechanism with which man finds himself endowed and which evidently serves more or less for knowing. But knowing is in itself not a faculty, a gift or a mechanism; on the contrary, it is a task which man imposes on himself. And a task which perhaps is impossible. In no way is knowing an instinct.

We use our faculties in order to know, not through a

simple desire to exercise them, but as an aid in a need we feel, a need which has nothing to do with those faculties and for which they may be neither adequate nor sufficient. Note, then, that knowing is not merely a matter of exercising the intellectual faculties, for it is not said that man manages to know; the only thing which is a fact is that he struggles painfully to know, that he inquires about *being* as the transcendence of appearance and exerts himself to apprehend it.

The real question about the origin of knowledge has always been denigrated by replacing it with an investigation of its mechanisms. Having an apparatus is not enough to assure that it will be used. Our houses are full of tools that are unused because what they give us no longer interests us. Juan is a man with a great talent for mathematics, but as only literature interests him, he does no mathematics. Moreover, as I have indicated, it is not at all certain that man's intellectual powers allow him to know. If by man's "nature" we understand, as did Aristotle, the combination of his bodily and mental endowments and their functioning, we will have to recognize that knowledge is not "natural" to him. On the contrary, when he makes use of all those mechanisms, one finds that he does not completely achieve what is proposed by the words "to know." His proposal, his cognitive eagerness, transcend his gifts, his means of satisfying it. He tries all the tools in his possession without getting full satisfaction out of any one of them, nor out of all of them together. The reality is that man has a strange urge to know, and that his powers—what Aristotle calls his nature—fail him.

This forces us, with no alternative, to recognize that the true nature of man is very broad and that it consists of the possession of powers, but also of deficiencies. Man is composed of what he has and what he lacks. If he uses his intellectual gifts in long and desperate effort, this is not simply because he has those powers, but on the contrary because he finds himself needing something he lacks, and in order to get it, he mobilizes all the means he possesses. The most fundamental error of all theories of knowledge has been the failure to note the initial incongruence between man's need to know and the "faculties" on which he counts to supply this need. Only Plato glimpsed the fact that the root of knowing, its very substance we might say, lies in the insufficiency of human powers, in the terrible fact that man "does not know." Neither God nor animal is in this condition. God knows everything, and therefore feels no need to know. The animal knows nothing. But man is the living insufficient one. Man needs to know, he is desperately aware that he is ignorant. This is what it is useful to analyze. Why does man's ignorance hurt him, how can he feel the ache in a member he never had?

4

Knowledge of the Universe or the Multi-verse. Technical Problems and Practical Problems. Panlogic and *Raison Vital*.

LIKE the flowing waters of the Guadiana River, this course in philosophy sprang up in one spot, then disappeared under desert sands, and finally came to light here. From my first lecture at the University I have here salvaged, as one does in catastrophes or sudden fires, only two points. One was spelled out in the title of this course; the other, which I would like from time to time to recall to you, is my proposal not to follow a straight line but to develop my thought in successive circles of a shortening radius, hence in a spiral curve. This allows us, indeed obliges us, to present each question first in the form which is most popular, least rigorous but most understandable, certain that we will find it treated later with more energy and more formality in a narrower circle. Thus, I said, many things which at first appearance may look to be merely a phrase or a triviality will reappear another time, improved by fortune, wearing a face which is graver and more fundamental.

With what was said earlier we finished our first swing of the spiral. Now we must begin what Plato would

call τὸν ἡμέτηρον δεύτερον πλοῦν—our second circumnaviga-
tion. We glimpsed the fact that scientific truth—the
truth of physics—has the admirable quality of being
exact, but is incomplete and penultimate. It is not sufficient unto itself. Its object is partial, it is only a piece of
the world and moreover it stems from many assumptions
which it presents without more ado as good; therefore
it does not stand on its own feet, does not have its base
and root within itself, is not a fundamental truth. For
this reason it seeks to integrate itself with other truths
which, being neither physical nor scientific, may be
complete and truly final. Where physics ends, the problem does not end; the man who stands behind the
scientist needs a truth that is whole and complete;
whether he likes it or not, by the very make-up of his
life a concept of the Universe is formed which is total.

Here we see two types of truth clearly counterpoised;
the scientific and the philosophic. The former is exact
but insufficient, the latter is sufficient but inexact. The
result is that the latter, that which is inexact, is a more
basic truth than the former; therefore it is a truth of
higher rank not only because its theme is broader, but
even as a type of knowledge; in short, the inexact
philosophic truth is a truer truth.

But this should not seem strange. The popular tendency to consider exactitude as an attribute which affects
the value of truth lacks both justification and meaning.
Exactness cannot exist except in terms of quantitative
objects, or as Decartes says, of *quod recepit magis et
minus,* that which is counted and measured. Therefore
it is not, strictly speaking, an attribute of the truth as
such, but only of certain specific things which exist in
the Universe; to be precise, only of quantity, and then,
with a value which is only approximate, of matter. A

truth may be very exact, and yet be a very small truth. For example, almost all the laws of physics are expressed in a most exact form, but as they are obtained by a calculation which is merely statistical, that is to say, by a calculation of probability, they have a value which is merely probable. The curious case is cited—and the theme merits separate treatment, being a burning and a most serious one—that as physics has been growing more and more exact, the physicists have been converting it more and more into a system of mere probabilities; therefore of second-class truths, of quasi-truths. The consequence of this leads modern physicists, those gigantic creators of an entirely new cosmic panorama, to occupy themselves with philosophy in order to set the truth peculiar to their profession within a more complete and vital truth.

We have made a first contact with a basic fact, with the fact which above all others makes up our lives and their horizon which is this world. This contact was still exceedingly imprecise and devoid of evidence. It seemed hardly more than a vague reaction, rather in the realm of poetry or pathos. Nevertheless it suggests enough so that we can glimpse the trajectory that lies ahead for us.

The philosophy of 1880 aspired at most to act as complement to the individual sciences. When these latter reached the point where they still could not obtain clear truths, they charged poor philosophy, like a maid-of-all-work, to finish the task with a series of vague and solemn pronouncements. Man was installing himself within physics, and where physics stopped, the philosopher went on straight ahead as though by inertia, using a kind of extramural physics to explain what remained. This physics over and beyond physics was metaphysics— therefore a physics outside itself. (Modern English philosophy, in the works of Russell or Whitehead, is still this.)

But what was said earlier shows that our road lies in an opposite direction. We insist that the physicist, and by the same token the mathematician, the historian, the artist, the politician—on seeing the limits of his craft, shall pull back within himself. Then he finds that he himself is not solely a physicist, but that physics is only one among an innumerable series of things which he does in his man's life. At the bottom of his being, in his deepest stratum, the physicist turns out to be a man, he is a human life. And this human life is inevitably and constantly submitting itself to an integrated world, to the Universe. Before being a physicist, he is a man, and being a man, he is preoccupied with the Universe, that is to say, he philosophizes, well or poorly, spontaneously or with a care for technique, in a fashion which may be barbarous or may be cultivated. Ours will not be the road that leads over and beyond physics; on the contrary, it will draw back from physics to basic life and find the root of philosophy here. The result will not be metaphysical but ante-physical. It is born out of life itself, and as we will see clearly, life cannot avoid philosophizing, no matter in how elemental a form. Therefore the first reply to our question, "what is philosophy?" may be phrased thus—"Philosophy is—a thing which is inevitable."

I promised the other day to answer that question "What is philosophy?" by listing a series of attributes, notes and features which would outline the profile of philosophic thoughts—but time, that great reaper, cut off my lecture just when the concept that we were seeking had begun to develop. I had to end my argument as best I could when the clock's hand stopped me.

But if you will think back, you will note that we had scarcely crossed the threshold of the matter; now we must enter into what lies within. We were trying to define philosophy as knowledge of the Universe, but at that point I put you on your guard lest this definition should mislead us and permit that which is essential and specific in the intellectual method called Philosophy to escape us. Strictly speaking, this danger arises not out of the definition itself, which is correct, but from the manner in which we men, especially those of the warm races, are accustomed to read and to listen. After a quarter of a century of production in the realm of ideas (I do not claim to be an ancient, but it happens that I began to publish at the age of eighteen), I have lost all illusion, all hope that either Spaniards or Argentinians will, with rare exceptions, understand the act of reading or of listening as more than a slipping along from the spontaneous or impressionist sense of one word to another, from the simplest meaning of one phrase to that of the next. Well then, this—and have no doubt of it—is no way to understand any philosophic expression.

Philosophy cannot be read, it must be de-read—that is, one must re-think each phrase, and this assumes that you break it into the words which form its ingredients; you then take each one of them, and instead of resting content with surveying its agreeable surface, you must throw yourself headlong into it, submerge yourself in it, go down into the depths of its meaning, look well to its anatomy and its boundaries in order to emerge again into the free air as master of its secret heart. When one does this with all the words of a sentence, they stay united not side by side, but subterraneously, joined by the very roots of their ideas; only then do they truly compose a philosophic phrase. For horizontal reading, the kind that slips along, for simple mental skating down the page, one must substitute vertical reading, immersion in the small abyss which is each word, a fruitful dive without a diving bell.

So I will try to install you successively within each of the terms which make up that definition. Having to repeat what was said in order to resume our ideological path, we can reaffirm what has already been stated and enrich it. It is important to do this, for the analysis is completely new, and I hope more rigorous than the more familiar ones.

And now for our task. The name of the thing for whose investigation philosophy was born is the Universe. This object, the Universe, is so strange, so radically different from all other objects, that the philosopher must at once station himself before it in an intellectual attitude which is completely different from that of the individual sciences confronting their own subjects of investigation.

By "Universe" I understand formally "everything there is." This means that the philosopher is not interested in each thing that exists, in its separate end, one might say, its private existence, but in the aggregate of all there is; consequently in everything which makes up that aggregate, and consequently in that aspect of each thing insofar as it concerns the others, its place, role and nature in the entirety of things—the public life of each thing, so to speak, what it is worth, what it represents in the sovereign scope of universal existence. By "things" we mean not only the real physical or living things, but also the unreal, the ideal and the fantastic, the transreal, if there be such things. Therefore I choose the verb "to be"; * I will not even say "all that exists," but "all there is." This phrase "there is" creates the widest circle of objects that can be drawn, even to the inclusion of things of which one must say that they are, but that they do not exist. Thus, for example, the squared circle, the knife without blade or haft, or all those marvelous beings of which the poet Mallarmé tells us—like the sublime hour which, he says, is the hour beyond the clock's face, or the best of women who is the "woman who is not a woman." Of the squared circle we can only say that it does not exist, because its existence is impossible; yet in order to pronounce on the poor squared circle so cruel a sentence, we must previously have contemplated it—in some sense it must have been.

I said before that the mathematician or the physicist begins by delimiting his object, by defining it, and this definition of the numerical, the group, or however mathematics chooses to begin (and the same is true with physics insofar as matter is concerned), contains the most essential attributes of the matter.

The individual sciences begin by dividing their problem and paring it down; to do this they start by knowing, or believing that they know, the most important aspect of it in advance. Their task is reduced to investigating the interior structure of its object, its fine innermost texture, we might say its histology. On the other hand, when the philosopher sets out on the search for all there is, he accepts a problem which is fundamental, an absolute problem, a problem without metes or bounds. Of that which he seeks—the Universe—he knows nothing.

Let us define precisely what it is of which he is

---

* The Spanish tongue has three verbs which in English must be translated by the single verb "to be." [Translator's note]

ignorant—to do this is to define most carefully the strangest, the unparalleled aspect of philosophy's problem.

First. When we ask ourselves what "all there is" includes, we have not the least suspicion of what this "all" will be. The only thing we know beforehand is that there is this, that, and the other thing, which is precisely what we are not looking for. We hunt the whole, and what we have is always that which is not the whole. Of this entirety we know nothing, and perhaps, among all those parts we already have, we lack the very ones which are most important to us, the most important of "all there is."

Second. But we also do not know whether that "all there is" will actually be a whole, that is to say, the Universe, or if perchance "whatever there is" makes up diverse wholes, that is to say, a Multi-verse.

Third. But we are further ignorant. Whether "whatever there is" forms a Universe or a Multi-verse, we do not know, nor do we know, as we set forth on our intellectual enterprise, whether or not it will be basically knowable, whether our problem will be solvable or not. *I beg you not to pass lightly over what I have just said.* It constitutes the strangest dimension of philosophic thought, the one that gives it a character all its own, that best differentiates the intellectual philosophic mode of thought from all the others.

The individual science does not doubt that its object is knowable—it will doubt whether it is fully knowable, and within its general problem will find certain special ones which it cannot resolve, including those which, as in mathematics, it will demonstrate as insoluble. But the attitude of the scientist implies faith in the possibility of coming to know its object. And this not merely a vague human confidence, but a constituent part of science itself, so inherent that when it defines its problem this is one and the same thing as determining the general method of solving it.

Or to put it another way: for the physicist a problem is that which in principle can be solved; to him the solution is in a way anterior to the problem; it is understood that the treatment which the problem tolerates is what will be called solution and knowledge. For example, concerning color, sound, and changes perceptible to the senses, the physicist can know only the quantitative relations and even these—the situations in time and in space—only relatively; even these relativities he can know only with the approximation which our senses and the available apparatus permit. This result, in theory so far from satisfactory, the physicist will call solution and knowledge. On the other hand, he will consider as a physical problem only that which can be submitted to measurements, and which accepts that methodic treatment.

It is only the philosopher who includes as an essential ingredient of his cognitive attitude the possibility that his object may turn out to be unknowable. And this means that philosophy is the sole science which takes the problem as it is presented, without any previous taming; unlike the circus hand who drugs his lions before entering their cage, philosophy hunts the wild beast in the jungle where it lives.

So the problem of philosophy is not only limitless in extent, since it embraces everything and has no boundaries, but also it is problematical in intensity; not only is it a problem of the absolute, but it is absolutely a problem. When, on the other hand, we say that the individual sciences deal with a problem which is relative or partial, we not only suggest that they are occupying themselves exclusively with a mere piece of the Universe, but also that that problem itself leans on data which are given as known and resolved, and is therefore only in part a problem.

In my judgment this is the moment to make a basic observation which, strangely enough, I have never before expressed. When one speaks of our cognitive or theoretic activity, it is defined very exactly as the mental operation which moves from the awareness of a problem to the achievement of a solution. The bad part about it is that one tends not to consider as important in this operation any stage but the last—the treatment and solution of the problem. Therefore, when one thinks about a science one is apt to see it as a repertory of solutions. I find this a mistake. In the first place, because speaking strictly and avoiding utopianism, as the temper of our time requires, it is very debatable if any problem has ever been fully resolved; therefore, in defining a science, the proper place for emphasis is not on the solutions it reaches. In the second place, a science is a process which is always fluid and open in the direction of solution; not an arrival at a long-desired coast, but a stormy course of navigation toward it. In the third and definitive place, one forgets that when a theoretic activity becomes an operation, and a moving from the awareness of a problem toward its solution, the primary thing is that awareness of the problem.

Why is this left aside as though it were an insignificant detail? Why does it seem natural, and not a matter for special thought, that man should have problems? Yet it is clearly obvious that the problem is the heart and nucleus of any science. All the rest is secondary to it. If we could nibble for a moment at the intellectual pleasure which paradox always brings, we would say that the only thing in a science which is not problematical is its problem; all the rest, and especially the solution of that problem, is precarious, arguable, shifting and changing. Each science is primarily a system of problems which are invariable or of very limited variation, and it is that treasure-house of problems which travels the length of the generations, passes from one mind to another, and in the long history of a science constitutes at once the patrimony and the safeguard of tradition.

But all this serves merely as a step toward a more basic consideration. The error suffered when one sees theoretic activity in terms of its solution, and not of its beginning, which is the problem itself, arises out of ignorance of what a marvel it is that man should have problems. The trouble is that most people do not distinguish between two different meanings of this word. Life poses problems for man, and always has; but these problems, which are not of his making but fall on him from the outside, posed for him by the very act of his living—these are the practical problems.

Let us try to define the mental attitude in which a practical problem appears. We are all of us surrounded, hemmed in, submerged by the cosmic reality within which we move. Suddenly we feel a compulsion or a desire which demands a very different surrounding reality; a rock, for instance, blocks our advance along the road. The practical problem consists in substituting a new surrounding reality for the existing one—in this instance a road which is free from rocks; this means creating something not now there. The practical problem is that mental attitude in which we plan to modify reality, consider giving being to something that does not yet exist but would be more convenient for us if it did.

This attitude is very different from the one in which

a theoretical problem arises. The usual expression of the problem is the question "*What* is this or that thing?" Note the strangeness of this mental act. That thing about which we ask "What is it?" is there, in one sense or another it has being; otherwise it would never occur to us to ask about it. But it follows that we are not content that it exists and is there—on the contrary, we are disturbed that it is there, and is of this or that kind; its existence irritates us. Why? Obviously because what it is, as it is, is not sufficient in itself; on the contrary we see that if it is only what it seems to be, if there is nothing else behind its appearance which completes it and supports it, its being is incomprehensible; or to put it another way, its being is not a being but a pseudo-being, something which ought not to be. Hence there is no theoretic problem unless it proceeds from what exists, what is indisputably there, but which nonetheless is thought of as not existing, as though it ought not to be. Theory, then, and let us emphasize the extravagance of this— begins by denying reality, by virtually destroying, annihilating the world; the ideal is to draw the world back into nothingness, to what it was before creation, since it is surprising that it exists, and the aim is to trace again the path of its genesis. If, then, the practical problem consists of making what is into what is not, but would be convenient if it were, the theoretic problem consists in making what is not into what is, and which in its present form irritates the intellect with its insufficiency.

For me, this audacity which leads man to deny a being provisionally and by denying it to convert it into a problem, is characteristic of and essential to all theoretic activity—which, by the same token, I regard as not reducible to any practical end whatsoever. This means that within the biological and utilitarian man there is another man, daring and sportive, who, rather than making life easy for himself by exploiting the real, complicates it by replacing the world's tranquility with the restlessness of problems. This basic leaning toward theory on the part of the human being we find to be an ultimate fact in the cosmos; it is vain to try to explain this as a consequence of the utilitarian principle that is used in understanding almost all the other phenomena of our living organism. Do not tell yourselves that it is necessity or some practical problem which obliges us to pose theoretic problems to ourselves. Why does this not happen to the animal, which undoubtedly has certain practical problems and is aware of them? Both kinds of problems have origins that are fundamentally different, and they cannot be reduced to any mutual status whatsoever. And vice versa, a being without desire, without needs, without appetites—a being that was only intellect and would have problems that were purely theoretic—would never come to perceive a problem which was practical.

Having made this basic observation, we apply it at once to our study of what philosophy is and we say, if the essential attribute of *homo theoreticus*, in his cognitive activity, is his gift of converting things into problems, in discovering his latent ontological tragedy, then there is no doubt that the theoretical attitude will be purer in proportion as the problem is more of a problem, and vice versa; when a problem is partial, the science concerned with it keeps a trace of the practical attitude, of blind utilitarianism, of an itch for action rather than for pure contemplation. Pure contemplation is only *theory* and at root it means exactly that.

Because philosophy's problem is the only absolute problem, the only pure fundamentally theoretic attitude is philosophy's attitude. It is knowledge carried to its maximum effort, it is intellectual heroism. The philosopher leaves nothing beneath his feet to serve as a comfortable support, as unshakable *terra firma*. He renounces all previous security, puts himself into absolute peril, practices the sacrifice of all his ingenuous beliefs, commits suicide as a live man in order to be reborn as if transfigured into pure exercise of intellect. He can say as did Francis of Assisi, "I need little, and that little I need very little." Or as Fichte said, *"Philosphieren heisst eigentlich nicht leben, leben heisst eigentlich nicht philosophieren."*—"Philosophy properly speaking is not living, and living, properly speaking, is not philosophizing." Nevertheless, we will see in what new and essential sense philosophy, at least my philosophy, does include life.

This problem of ours was a problem in the absolute sense because it began by admitting its possible insolubility; perhaps, we said, the Universe or whatever there may be is unknowable. And it may be unknowable for two different reasons. One of them lies in the possibility that our capacity for knowing may be limited, as positivism, relativism, and criticism in general believe. But there is also the chance that the Universe may be unknowable for a reason which the familiar theories of knowledge ignore—because even though our intelligence may be without limits, the world, the state of being, the Universe in itself, in its own texture, may be opaque to thought because in itself it may be irrational.

Until these last few years no one has tried to pose the problem of knowledge again in the high and classic form. Kant himself, who was a most acute genius, and of permanent value in that portion of the problem on which he worked, perhaps did more than any one else to prevent it from being seen in its entirety. Today we are beginning to find it strange and unacceptable that even when the problem of knowledge is treated in that partial form there should be a desire to elude the general question. If I ask myself what and how much the subject man can know, I need first to find out what it is that I understand by knowledge, no matter who does the knowing. Only thus will I be able to see whether in man's particular case, the generic conditions are fulfilled without which any knowledge is impossible. Today, especially since the recent book of the great German thinker Nicolai Hartmann, we begin to recognize that one must start by determining what are the primary conditions of knowledgeability. In its simplest definition, knowledge was that famous and trivial *adaequatio rei et intellectus*, that is, a mutual state of assimilation as between thinking and being. But we have already seen that a minimum of *adaequatio* was enough to give a merely symbolic knowledge in which my thought of a reality has almost no likeness to that reality, as one language shows words which are different from those of another, and we rest content with corresponding or parallel meanings. There could, of course, be no correspondence between two different languages if they did not have, in the last analysis, a common formal structure, that is to say, a grammatical skeleton which was, at least in part, common to both of them.

The same thing is true of knowledge: even in the simplest there must be at least a minimum of effective assimilation as between the thing known and the thinking process, or the subjective state of the one who knows. The world can enter into my mind only if there is some coincidence between the structure of my mind and the structure of the world, if my thinking behaves more or less coincidentally with the world's being. Thus the old scholastic expression takes on a new and far more serious meaning. I am not considering the meaning it has had up to now, an almost frivolous meaning, namely, that if the intellect knows a thing it takes on a semblance of the thing, that is, it copies the thing; what concerns us now is the deeper condition without which even this would not be possible. As a matter of fact, my thought cannot copy the reality, cannot receive this within itself unless the reality in turn bears some likeness to my thinking. Now then, and this formula also I believe to be new, the *adaequatio* between both terms must be mutual; there must be a coincidence between my thought and the thing, but this is possible only if the thing in itself coincides with the structure of my thought.

Thus, every theory of knowledge, unconsciously and perhaps unwillingly, would have been an ontology (a science of the study of knowledge)—that is to say, a doctrine concerned on the one hand with what the being is, and on the other what the thinking about it (a being or a particular thing) is, and then making a comparison between the two. Consequently thinking was sometimes discovered to be a result of being—this was realism— and at other times it was shown that the structure of being proceeded from the very act of thinking—and this was idealism. But in both cases there was an understanding, somewhat less than conscious, that in order to justify knowledge the structural identity of both terms must be demonstrated. Thus Kant sums up his whole *Critique of Pure Reason* in these words which, although bristling with technicalities, contain in my judgment the most humble, naked and perfect clarity: "The conditions of the possibility of experience [or thought] *are the same* as the conditions of the possibility of the objects [read being, or reality]."

Only in this way, I repeat, can one attack in all seriousness the problem of knowledge, in all its ideal and frightening drama. It may be that the structure of being coincides completely with that of thinking, that is, that being is of the same nature and function as thinking. This is the great thesis of rationalism—the height of gnosiological optimism. If this were so, thought could reach knowledge merely by thinking about itself, sure that any reality outside it (obeying the same laws as thinking, or logos) would coincide with the results of thought's internal analysis. Hence Aristotle makes God, the principle of the Universe, consist solely of thinking about thinking—*noesis noeseos*—He knows His Universe solely by thinking about Himself. According to this, reality consists of logical matter, the real is the rational, as that other rationalist, the *panlogist* Hegel, will say at the other extreme of the history of philosophy. If we want to catch this fashion of philosophizing off balance, let us cite certain words of Leibnitz toward the end of his *New Essays on Human Understanding*. The great optimist says, "*Je ne conçois les choses inconnues ou confusément connues que de la manière de celles qui nous sont distinctement connues.*" This man is sure that the unknown, that which is real but beyond our thought, will have a manner of being, a composition equivalent to the real which is already known; that is, that portion of reality whose consistence already coincides with that of our thinking. For me, this is a classic example of what I call intellectual utopism, that is to say, the mad faith that thought, when it wishes to penetrate the real at almost any spot—*u-topos*—on its infinite body will find that body transparent and coinciding with thought itself. If this is so, I need not wait to find the unknown real; having anticipated it, I know how it will behave.

Opposed to this champion of optimism let us put the skeptical extremist—for whom being does not coincide in the least with thinking, and who therefore regards all knowledge as impossible. And in between we will establish the position which seems most discreet, namely that in which one thinks he sees that only in part does being coincide with thinking, that there are only certain objects which behave as thinking behaves, that is, logically. A theory of knowledge governed by this third point of view will be careful to trace very sharp and true the line of coincidences and discrepancies between thought and the Universe, will draw a map of the objective showing both the civil zones of the world which thinking can penetrate, and the impenetrable, irrational zones. For example, numbers form a class of objects which are coincident with the logos to so great an extent that men have believed it possible to rationalize all mathematics and construct it purely with logic.

But we are now living through one of the greatest and most glorious battles of the intellect which have ever taken place; this with modern physics will, in the long parade of the years, render our day noble. I refer to the attempt made by Brouwer and Weyl to demonstrate the partial discrepancy between the consistency of numbers and that of concepts; therefore, the impossibility of a logical or formalist mathematics, and the necessity of a mathematics which is faithful to the peculiarity of its object which they call "intuitionist," a mathematics which would not be logical, but strictly mathematical.

If we go from mathematics on to more complicated things—physical matter, organic life, psychic life, social life, historic life—the proportion of irrationality or of impenetrability to pure thinking increases; it is most probable that where the object under consideration is no less than the Universe, that part of it which is rebellious and unintelligible if approached through the pure traditional *logos* would be at a maximum. In physics, reason still moves along comfortably enough, but as Bergson says admirably—though from motives which are less admirable—". . . apart from physics reason must be inspected by good sense." What Bergson calls "good sense" is what I have called very formally "vital reason," a reason broader than good sense, for which many objects are rational that, in terms of the old *raison*—conceptual reason or pure reason—are in effect irrational.

But also it would hardly be intelligent to interpret the definition of philosophy as a doctrine of the Universe, and the tendency to construct a *maximum* of philosophic *corpus* as an ingenuous lapse into the old metaphysics. These external objections, whether political, pedagogic, or hygienic, to a thought which moves forward by virtue of internal reasons, are always childish, frivolous, and lacking in theoretic veracity. In general, every one who attacks a work of theory for motives which are alien to it, and by means of *argumenta hominis ad hominem*, automatically declares his lack of ability as a man of theory. It is not worthwhile to talk of things to their faces without going into them, there is no value in the *vorbeireden* in which one eludes the very questions on which one pretends to express judgments. I would urge the new generations of Spanish intellectuals that on this point they be more than ever urgent, for that is the essential condition through which a country takes on a serious reputation and acquires a true intellectual life. "The rest is," as a character in a Spanish novel says, "no more than carriage paint."

A philosophy as we have seen it defined, and one for which it is essential to admit in advance that its object may possibly be unknowable, can be bad; so also can be an ingenuous lapse into the old metaphysics. So far as I know, the philosophic point of departure has never been given an expression more demanding of criticism and caution. But we who are faithful to the heroic way of knowing and thinking which, like it or not, is the essence of philosophy, cannot content ourselves with being cautious, but must be complete. Caution, then, but without suspicion; just naturally cautious. There is no need to stand before the Universe as suspicious as a villager. Positivism was a small-town type of philosophy. As Hegel said, "The fear of error is already an error, and if it is analyzed there will be revealed in its depths a fear of the truth." The philosopher who is prepared for the maximum degree of intellectual danger, who expounds his whole thought, is under an obligation to exercise full liberty—to free himself from everything, including that rustic suspicion in the face of a possible metaphysics. So we do not renounce any critical strictness; on the contrary, we carry it to the necessary extreme but we do it simply, giving ourselves no air of importance on this account, declining to act the critic. Like all our contemporaries, we detest the vain and exaggerated attitude, the piling-up of useless gestures. Above all, one must be what one is, without display, in sober honesty, evading all temptation to parade oneself as an exaggerated figure-head.

If, in order not to go astray, we now grasp Ariadne's thread, which must be done in every development of concepts, we can sum up what has been said by repeating its first formula, which now will have more meaning for you. Philosophy is knowledge of the Universe, or of everything there is, but when we set forth on its quest we know neither what there is, nor if what there is forms a Universe or a Multi-verse, nor whether Universe or Multi-verse will be knowable.

The enterprise, then, seems mad. Why undertake it? Would it not be more prudent to drop it, to dedicate oneself solely to living, and dispense with philosophizing? For the old Roman hero, on the contrary, it was necessary to navigate but it was not necessary to live. Man will always be divided into two classes, of whom the better will find the superfluous to be the most necessary. In the small Oriental patio there rises, sweet and tremulous as the slender thread of the fountain, the voice of Christ, who warns, "Martha, Martha, only one thing is needful." And with this, facing the busy and useful Martha, he alludes to Mary, loving and superfluous.

5

The Need for Philosophy. Present and Compresent. The Fundamental Being. Autonomy and Pantonomy. Defense of the Theologian vis-à-vis the Mystic.

ON stating the problem of philosophy we found it to be the most radical, most fundamental problem that could be imagined, the very archetype of problems. On the other hand, we saw that the more problematical a problem is, the purer is the cognitive, theoretic attitude which perceives and scrutinizes it. Hence, philosophy is the intellectual exercise par excellence; compared with it, all the other sciences, including pure mathematics, hold a vestige of the practical.

But this same purity, this superlative degree of intellectual heroism which infuses philosophy—does it not give this discipline a somewhat monstrous and even frenetic character? Is there good sense in setting oneself a problem as extraordinary as is the philosophic problem? In terms of probabilities, one must admit that success in that undertaking called philosophy is the least probable in all the world. It seems, I said, a mad enterprise. Why try it? Why not content oneself with living and let philosophizing go? If success in its pursuit is not probable, then philosophy is of no use, there is no need for it.

Agreed: yet it is a fact that there are men for whom the superfluous is the necessary. And let us remember the divine opposition between the useful Martha and the superfluous Mary. The truth is—and it is to this that the words of Christ allude—that such a sharp duality does not exist; life itself, including organic or biological life, is, in the last analysis, not to be understood in terms of utility alone, and can only be explained as an infinite phenomenon of a somewhat sportive character.

And so that vital exercise which is called philosophizing—is it necessary? Is it not necessary? If by "necessary" one means "to be useful" for something else, philosophy is at least not of primary necessity. But the degree of necessity possessed by that which is useful is only relative, relative to its end. The true necessity is what every being feels for being what it is—the bird for flying, the fish for swimming, and the intellect for philosophizing. This need to exercise the function or the act which defines us is at once the highest and the most essential need. Hence Aristotle did not hesitate to say about the sciences *anankaioterai pasai, aimeinon d' oudemia*—(*Metaphysics* 983–10): "They are all of them most necessary, but no one of them is superior." And Plato, seeking the boldest definition of philosophy, in the final hour of his most rigorous thinking, in the full tide of dialogue of the *Sophist* will say that philosophy is *he episteme ton eleutheron* or in exact translation, the sportive science. What would have happened to Plato if he had said that here? And if, in addition, he had given his dissertation in a public gymnasium where the young elegants of Athens, attracted by Socrates' round head, clustered around his words like moths around a lantern and leaned toward him their long Discobolus necks?

But let us leave our friend Plato and go on scrutinizing our friend the truth.

Philosophy does not spring forth for reasons of utility, but neither does it flourish out of caprice. It is constitutionally necessary to the intellect. Why? Its purpose was to seek all things as such, to hunt the Unicorn, to capture the Universe. But why that eagerness? Why not be content without philosophizing, with what we find in the world, with what already is, what stands there clear before us? For this simple reason: all that there is, there in front of us, given to us, present and clear, is in its very essence a mere piece, a bit, a fragment, the stump of something absent. And we cannot see it without sensing and missing the part that is not there. In every given being, every datum of the world, we find its essential fracture line, its character as a part and only a part; we see the scar of its ontological mutilation; its ache of the amputated cries out at us, its nostalgia for the bit that is lacking, its divine discontent. Some years ago, speaking in Buenos Aires, I defined discontent as "like loving without being loved, like a pain we feel in parts we do not have." It is the missing of what we are not, the recognizing of ourselves as crippled and incomplete.

Strictly speaking, what I want to say is as follows:

If we take any object among those we find in the world, and focus on what we have when we hold it in front of us, we will very shortly realize that it is only a fragment, and that being a fragment, it forces us to think of something else which would complete it. Thus the colors we see, which are always set so gay and gallant before our eyes, are not just what they seem to those eyes; that is, they are not only colors. Every color needs more or less to extend itself; it exists, it is poured out *in extenso;* there is no color without extension. It is only one part of the whole which we might call colored expansion, or expanded color. But this extension, in turn, cannot be only colored extension. In order to be what it is it presupposes a thing which is extended, something which sustains both the extension and the color, an understratum or a support. As Leibnitz said concerning Descartes, extension requires something of *extensione prius.* Let us, as is traditional, call that support for color by the name of matter.

On arriving at matter we seem finally to have reached something which is sufficient unto itself. Matter does not need to be upheld by anything; there it is, by itself, not like color, which exists by virtue of something else and thanks to the matter which sustains it. But at this point suspicion arises; if matter, once existent, is sufficient unto itself, it could nevertheless not give to itself being, nor could it come into being through any capacity of its own. One cannot think of matter without seeing it as something brought into existence by another power, just as one cannot see the arrow in the air without looking for the hand that launched it. So matter, too, is a part of a larger process which produced it, of a broader reality which completes it. All this is trivial, and I use it merely to clarify the idea with which we are dealing.

This other example seems to me clearer and closer. In our perception of this room the whole of it is present. To our vision, at least, it seems a thing which is complete and sufficient. It is composed of what we see in it, and of nothing else. At least if we analyze what is in our perception when we see it, there seems to be nothing more than its colors, its lights, its forms, its space, and nothing more seems to be needed. But if, on leaving it, we were to find that at its door the world ended, that outside this room there was nothing, not even empty space, our minds would suffer a shock of surprise. But why? If there was no more of this room in our minds than what we see, why should we be immediately surprised if there were nothing around it of house, street, city, earth, atmosphere and so on? Apparently there was in our perception, along with the immediate presence of the room's interior which we see, a background, though vague and latent, and if this were lacking we would miss it. That is to say, even in the simple act of perception this room was not a thing complete, but only a foreground standing against a vaguely noted background on which we counted, a background that though hidden and somehow attached did exist for us, enfolding what we in fact see. That vague, enfolding background is not now present, but is compresent. And in fact always when we see something, this something is presented against a latent background—obscure, enormous, undefined in its contours—which is simply the world, the world of which it forms a part, the world of which it is a piece. In every case what we see is only the visible promontory moved toward us by the latent rest of the world. And so we can lift this observation to the status of a general law and say that when a thing is present, the world is always compresent, always included with it.

The same thing happens if we fix our eyes on our own intimate reality, on that which is psychic. What we see of our interior being at any moment is only a small part —these ideas of which we are now thinking, this hurt that we suffer, this small image painted on our inner screen, this emotion we now feel. But this poor heap of things of ours that we see is only what our glance catches as it is turned inward, it is only, so to speak, like the shoulder of our complete and effective self, the rest of which remains in the background, as imposing as a great valley, or a mountain range so huge that at any given moment we see of it only the corner of a landscape.

Well then, the world—in the sense we are now giving the word—is only the conjunction of things which we can go on seeing one after the other. Those which we do not now see act as background for the ones we do see, but later it will be the others which we have before us, immediate, clear and provided for us. And if each one is only a fragment and the world is no more than a collection of these fragments, this means that the entire world in its turn—the combination of what is given us, and which, being given us, we can call "our world"— will also be a fragment, enormous, colossal, but a fragment and nothing more. Not even to itself does the world explain itself; on the contrary, when we find ourselves theoretically facing it, what is given us is only . . . a problem.

In what does the problematical aspect of the problem consist? Let us take the old example: the stick in the water appears straight to the sense of touch, but not straight to the sense of sight. The intellect would like to accept one of these appearances, but the other asserts equal rights. The intellect is anguished at not being able to depend on either of them and seeks a solution: it tries to save itself by calling them mere appearances. The consciousness of a being and a non-being, of a contradiction is the problem. As Hamlet said, "To be or not to be, that is the question."

In a similar fashion, the world that we find exists, but at the same time it is not sufficient unto itself, does not support its own being, cries out about what it lacks, proclaims its non-being and obliges us to philosophize; for this is what philosophizing is—seeking to give the world its integrity, completing it as a Universe, and out of the part constructing for it a whole in which it can lodge and be at rest. The world is a fragmentary and insufficient object, an object founded on something other than itself, something not given to it. Strictly speaking, this something has a founder's mission, it is the fundamental being. As Kant said, "When the conditional is given to us, the unconditional is posed before us as a problem." Here you have the decisive philosophic problem and the mental need which spurs us toward it.

Focus for a moment on the peculiar situation which is created for us when we confront that fundamental being which is postulated but not given. It is not enough to seek it as something in the world which has not thus far been made apparent to us, but which might perhaps manifest itself tomorrow. The fundamental being, by its very essence, is not a datum, is never a thing present to the understanding; it is the very thing that is lacking in all that is present. How do we know about it? When a piece of a mosaic is lacking, we recognize it by the hole which is left: what we see of it is its absence; its way of being present is to be absent. Similarly, the fundamental being is the eternal and essential absent one, that which is always lacking in the world—and of it we see only the scar which its absence has left, as on a cripple we see the arm that is not there. And one must define it by drawing the outline of the wound, describing the fracture line. In its role as a fundamental being it cannot resemble the given being which is, by very virtue of being given, secondary and established. The former, on the contrary, is in essence the completely other, the formally different, the absolutely exotic.

I think that rather than building illusions about the nearness of that fundamental being, and its likeness to the things that are given and well-known, one must emphasize its heterogeneous character and what it has that is different from and not to be compared with any intraworldly being. In this sense, although only in this, I sympathize with those who refuse to make the transcendental being familiar, domesticated, almost our neighbor. As what philosophy sees as a problem of the world's creation appears in the various religions under the name of God, there also we find two attitudes—that which would bring God too close, and like St. Theresa make Him walk amid the cooking pots, and that which—in my judgment with greater respect and more philosophic tact – sets Him apart and would skirt around Him.

In this context, I am always moved to remember the figure of Marcion, Christianity's first great founder of a heresy, whom the Church, though feeling bound to call him "first born of Satan," always treated (out of a fine conscience) with unusual consideration because he was, aside from questions of dogma, a man exemplary in all things. Like all gnostics, Marcion was moved by a conscience that was hypersensitive to the qualities of limitation, defect, insufficiency, which are ascribed to all mundane things. Therefore he does not admit that the true and supreme God had anything to do with the world; He is that which is absolutely different, distinct, and other than the world—He is *allotrios*. Otherwise He would be contaminated morally and ontologically with the world's imperfections and limitations. Hence, according to Marcion, the supreme and authentic God could not be a creator of the world: if He were, He would be the creator of the insufficient, and hence He Himself would be insufficient; concerning the world, we seek perfect sufficiency. To create something is, in the last analysis (I am now interpreting Marcion), to be contaminated by that which is created. God the Creator is a second power, the God of the Old Testament, a God who has much about Him of the intramundane, the God of justice and armies, which means that He is indissolubly linked with crime and struggle. On the other hand, the true God is not just, He is simply good; He is not justice but charity and love. He exists forever and apart from the world, remote from it, untouched by it; therefore we can only call Him "the stranger God," ξένος δεός, par excellence. But by the same token, as He is absolutely other than the world, He balances it, compensates for it and completes it—for the very reason that He has no part in the world He saves it. And for the gnostic this is the task which in the highest sense is divine; not to create the wicked world like a pagan demiurge, but on the contrary to "de-create" it, to nullify its constitutional evil—that is, to save it.

If, momentarily, we must emphasize that distinction, this is not enough. Gnosticism stops there; it is the exaggeration of that moment, of the *Deus exsuperantissimus*. But one must make the journey back. Do not conclude that I have confessed a leaning toward Marcionism. I could hardly do that inasmuch as that heresy talks of God, a problem of theology—this for us was only an illustration. We are talking only of the fundamental being, which is exclusively the subject of philosophy.

Philosophy is knowledge of the Universe, or of whatever there is. We have already seen that for the philosopher this implied the need to set for himself an absolute problem, that is to say, he cannot take as his point of departure the earlier beliefs, and cannot accept anything as known in advance. The known is what is no longer a problem. Well then, that which is known outside of,

apart from or previous to philosophy, is known from a
point of view which is partial and not universal, is knowing on an inferior level which is no help on the heights
where philosophic knowledge moves *a nativitate*. Seen
from philosophic heights, all other knowing has about it
a touch of the ingenuous and the relatively false, that is
to say, it again becomes problematical. Hence Nicolas
of Cusa called the sciences *docta ignorantia*.

This position of the philosopher, which accompanies
his extreme intellectual heroism and would be so uncomfortable if it did not bear with it his inevitable vocation, imposes on his thought what I call the imperative
of *autonomy*. This means renouncing the right to lean
on anything prior to the philosophy which he may be
creating, and pledging himself not to start from supposed
truths. Philosophy is a science without suppositions. I
understand by this a system of truths which has been
constructed without admitting as groundwork any truth
that is given as proven outside of that system. So there
is no philosophic admission which the philosopher does
not have to forge with his own means. Philosophy is an
intellectual law unto itself, it is self-contained. This I
call the principle of autonomy—and this links us directly
to the whole critical past of philosophy; it brings us back
to the great mover and shaker of modern thought and
qualifies us as the latest grandsons of Descartes. But have
no faith in the tenderness of grandsons. Tomorrow we
are going to cast up accounts with our grandfathers. The
philosopher begins by purging his spirit of received beliefs, by converting that spirit into a desert isle devoid of
truths, and then, a recluse on this island, he condemns
himself to a methodic procedure in the Robinson Crusoe
tradition. Such was the meaning of the methodical doubt
which places Descartes forever on the doorstep of philo-

sophic knowledge. Its meaning was not simply the
doubting of all that stirs doubt within us—every intelligent man does this continually—but it consists in
doubting even that which in fact is not doubted, but in
principle could be doubtful. This instrumental and
technical doubt, which is philosophy's scalpel, has a
radius of action far broader than man's habitual suspicion,
in that leaving behind it that which is doubtful, it moves
toward that which can be doubted. Hence Descartes did
not entitle his famous meditation *"De ce qu'on revoque
en doute"* but *"De ce qu'on peut revoquer en doute."*

Here you have the root of a characteristic aspect of all
philosophy—the paradoxical face that it wears. All philosophy is paradox; it stands apart from the natural
opinion which we use in daily life, because it considers
as theoretically doubtful the most primary and elemental
beliefs which in the process of living do not seem to us
at all questionable.

But once the philosopher, by virtue of the principle
of autonomy, has fallen back to those first truths in
which there is no room for doubt, even in theory, and
which for this reason prove and confirm themselves, he
must turn his face to the Universe, embrace it whole and
entire, and conquer it. That minimum point, or points,
of strict truth must be stretched like a rubber band to
encompass all there is. Opposed to this ascetic principle
of cautious retreat comprised in autonomy, there operates a contrary principle of tension: this is universalism,
the intellectual urge toward the whole, which I call
pantonomy.

The principle of autonomy, negative, static, and
cautious, inviting us to take care but not to move
ahead, which neither orients nor directs our advance,
is not enough. It is not enough merely to keep from

straying: one must make the right move, continue the attack on our problem without ceasing, and as our problem lies in defining the whole, the Universe, each philosophic concept will have to be fabricated with regard to the whole; this is in contrast to concepts of individual disciplines which are concerned with the part as an isolated part, or as a pretended whole. Thus physics tells us solemnly what matter is, as if there were in the whole Universe only matter, as if matter *were* the Universe. Hence physics has tended to vaunt itself as the authentic philosophy, and this subversive pseudophilosophy is materialism. The philosopher, on the other hand, will search for that value which matter has as a fragment of the Universe; he will tell the ultimate truth about each thing, and the part it has in the functioning of the whole. It is this conceptual principle which I call *pantonomy*, or the law of totality.

Ever since the Renaissance, the principle of autonomy has been abundantly proclaimed, at times with a regrettable emphasis on exclusiveness which checked philosophic thought to the point of paralysis. On the other hand, the principle of *pantonomy*, or universalism, won adequate attention in the ancient soul only at moments, and in the short period of romantic philosophy which runs from Kant to Hegel. I would go so far as to say that this, and only this, brings us close to the post-Kantian systems whose ideological style is otherwise so extraordinarily timeless. But this single coincidence is of great importance. We coincide with them in refusing to rest content with avoiding error, and in considering that the best way to succeed is not by narrowing the visual field but, on the contrary, by stretching it very widely, converting into an intellectual imperative a methodical principle, the proposal to think about everything and leave nothing outside. Since Hegel's day men have forgotten that philosophy is that complete and integral thought, and nothing else—with all its advantages and, naturally, with all its defects.

We want a philosophy which will be philosophy and nothing more, which accepts its destiny, with its splendor and its misery, and does not look enviously in all directions, seeking for itself the cognitive virtues which belong to other sciences, such as the exactness of mathematical truth or the verification by the senses and by practice which belong to physical truth. It was not by chance that the philosopher of the past century was so faithless to his creed. In the western world it was characteristic of those days not to accept one's destiny but to wish to be what one was not. Hence that was by nature a revolutionary age.

In the last analysis, "revolutionary spirit" means not only an urge to improve—which is always excellent and noble—but also an impulse to believe that one has a limitless ability to be what one is not, that one has only to think of the best possible order or condition of society or the world in order to attain it and make it real; not seeing that both society and the world have structures which are in essence beyond change. This limits the realization of our desires and gives a somewhat frivolous character to every attempt at reform that fails to recognize it. For the revolutionary spirit which tries in utopian fashion to make things what they can never be, nor would have any reason for being, we must substitute the great ethical principle which Pindar preached in terms of poetry, and say simply "Win through to being what you are."

Philosophy must rest content with being the poor little thing it is, leaving aside those graces which are not its own so that they may adorn other ways and kinds of knowing. Despite the megalomaniacal aspect which philosophy seems at first sight to present when it seeks to embrace and devour the Universe, this is a discipline which is neither more nor less modest than the others. Because the Universe, or all there is, is not *each one* of the things there are, but only the universal aspect of each thing, therefore only a facet of each thing. In this sense, but only this, the object of philosophy also is partial, in that it is the part through which each thing is inserted into the whole, what might be called its umbilical portion. And it would not be incongruous to assert that, when all is said and done, the philosopher too is a specialist, a specialist in universes.

But just as Einstein, as we have seen, makes of metrics, which is empirical and therefore relative (hence at first sight considered a limitation and even a principle of error)—the very beginning of all physical concepts, so philosophy (it is very important to emphasize this) makes of the intellectual ambition to embrace the Universe the logical and methodical beginning of its ideas. Hence out of what might seem a vice, or a mad ambition, it makes its austere fate and fruitful virtue. To those who are most discriminating in philosophic matters, it will seem strange that this imperative insistence on embracing the whole should be called a logical principle. Logic traditionally knows no principles but those of identity and contradiction, of sufficient reason and the excluded middle. So this concerns a type of heterodoxy which for the moment I merely ask you to note. Later, we will see the serious meaning and important reasons contained within this heterodoxy.

But we must still add to the concept of philosophy one new and very important attribute. An attribute which may seem too obvious to warrant formulating. Nevertheless, it is very important. We call philosophy a theoretic knowledge, a theory. A theory is a web of concepts—in the strict sense of the word *concept*. And this strict sense defines concept as a content of the mind which can be put into words. That which cannot be put into words, the unsayable or the ineffable, is not a concept; knowledge that consists of an ineffable vision of the object may be all you want, including, perhaps, the supreme form of knowledge, but it is not what we attempt under the name of philosophy. If we imagine a philosophic system like that of Plotinus or Bergson, which shows us by means of concepts that true knowledge is an ecstasy of the conscious in which the latter moves beyond the limits of the intellectual or the conceptual and makes immediate contact with reality, needing no mediation or intermediary action on the part of concept, we would say that these are philosophies insofar as they prove the need of ecstasy with non-ecstatic means, and that they cease to be philosophies when they leap from concept to immersion in the mystic trance.

Remember the impression of sincerity which is conveyed when one deals with the works of the mystics. The author invites us to a marvelous voyage, the most marvelous of all. He tells us that he has been in the very center of the Universe, in the heart of the absolute. He proposes that we retrace the path with him. Delighted, we prepare to depart and obediently to follow our guide. Yet we find ourselves a bit surprised that he who has been submerged in so prodigious a place and an element, in so decisive an abyss as is God or the Absolute or the One, has not been more upset, more taken aback, more dehumanized, that he appears not to be possessed of a new accent, different from the rest of us. When Theophile Gautier returned to Paris from his trip to Spain everybody saw it in his face, which was browned by the sun of the other side of the Pyrenees. According to the Breton legend, those who descended into St. Patrick's purgatory never laughed again. The rigidity of the facial muscles, those earnest workers for a smile, served to authenticate their subterranean excursion. But the mystic comes back intact, unaltered by the powerful matter which has been surrounding him. Yet if anyone tells us that he has come back from the bottom of the sea we look automatically at his clothing in the hope of finding caught within it bits of algae and coral, flora and fauna of the deep abyss.

But so great is the illusion offered by the proposed voyage that we put aside this momentary sense of strangeness and move resolute into the mystic's path. His words, his *logoi*, seduce us. The mystics have been the most formidable technicians of the word, the most exact writers. It is curious, and somewhat paradoxical, that in all the languages of the world it is the mystics who have been the classicists of the word. Portentous speakers, they have always had a great dramatic talent. Drama is the supernormal tension of our souls, produced by something announced to us as holding promise for the future; toward this we move step by step so that the curiosity, the terror, or the appetite which is aroused by that future is multiplied within itself, and heaped higher at each new moment. If the distance which separates us from that future, so attractive or so terrible, is divided into stages, each stage that we reach renews and augments our tension. He who is going to cross the Sahara desert is curious about its borders where civilization ends, but he is more curious about what lies within those borders, about what is already desert, and even more so about the desert's very center, as if this center contained the desert in superlative degree. In this way curiosity, rather than being satisfied as it is used, becomes like a muscle which is fed and developed by exercise. What comes after the first step is interesting, but the next thing is even more interesting, and so on successively. Every good dramatist knows the effect of an almost mechanical tension which is produced by this segmenting of the road toward an announced future. And therefore the mystics always divide their route toward ecstasy into what are virtually steps. Sometimes this appears as a castle divided into walls set one within the other, like those Japanese boxes which always have another box inside—this was Saint Theresa's way; at other times it is the ascent to a mountain, with subsidiary heights on the way, as with Saint John of the Cross, or a staircase where each step promises us a new vision and a new landscape, as with the spiritual ladder of St. John Climacus. Let us confess that when we arrive at each successive stage we suffer a certain disillusion: what we can see from it represents no great advance. But the hope that the next, when we reach it, will show us something new and magnificent keeps us courageous and alert.

But when we arrive at the last barrier, the final step, the summit of Mount Carmel, the mystic guide, who has not stopped talking for a single moment, says to us, "Now you stay here alone; I am going to plunge myself into ecstasy. When I return I will tell you about it." Docilely we wait, bound by the illusion that with our own eyes we will see the return of the mystic, straight out of the abyss, still dripping mysteries, with the sharp odor of the winds of over-there still clinging to his traveling clothes. Here he comes back—he approaches us and says, "Well, you know, I cannot tell you anything at all, for what I have seen is in itself ineffable, untellable, and not to be recounted." And the mystic, earlier so loquacious, so much the master of speech, at this decisive moment turns taciturn, or what is even worse and more frequent, brings us from the other world bits of news that are so trivial, so little interesting, that they tend to lower the prestige of the over-there. As the German proverb says, "When one takes a long trip one brings back something to talk about." The mystic, back from his other-worldly voyage, brings nothing, or almost nothing, to talk about. We have wasted our time. The classicist in language becomes a specialist in silence.

With this, I would like to suggest that the discreet attitude toward mysticism, in the strict sense of the term, ought not to include a pedantic attempt to study mystics as though they were cases in a psychiatric clinic —as if this would clarify anything essential in their work —or in offering certain earlier objections; on the contrary, let us accept whatever they propose and take them at their word. They pretend to arrive at a knowledge which is superior to reality. If the spoils in the form of wisdom which the trance yields them were actually worth more than theoretic knowledge we would not for a moment hesitate to abandon the latter and make mystics of ourselves. But what they tell us is trivial and insuperably monotonous. The mystics' reply is that knowledge gained in a state of ecstasy transcends all language and is by its very superiority a wordless knowledge. Only the individual by himself can arrive at it, and the mystic's book differs from a scientific book in that it is not a doctrine on transcendent reality, but a road map for finding that reality, a discourse on a method, an itinerary for the mind reaching toward the absolute. The mystic's knowledge is untransferable, and in essence silent.

Nor could one in truth put too much faith in this emphasis on the mute and untransferable character of certain types of knowledge as an objection to mysticism. The color that our eyes see and the sound that our ears hear are, in fact, unsayable. The peculiar hue of a real color cannot be expressed in words; one has to see it, and only he who sees it knows truly what it is like. The world's chromatic range, which is so plain to the rest of us, cannot be communicated to one who is utterly blind. It would, then, be a mistake to disdain what the mystic sees for the mere reason that only he can see it. One must root out of knowledge that curious "democracy" of knowing which would have us believe that the only existent thing is that which the whole world knows. No; there are men who can see more than the others do, and the others cannot properly do anything but accept that superiority when it becomes apparent. To put it another way, he who does not see must have faith in he who does.

But some will ask, "How can we prove that someone else does in fact see what we ourselves cannot see? The world is full of charlatans, of the vain, the deceitful, the mad." In this case the criterion does not seem to me hard to find; I will believe that someone sees more than I when that superior vision, invisible to me, gives him superiorities which are apparent to me. I judge by its effects. Note, then, that it is not the ineffable character of mystical knowing or the impossibility of transferring it that makes mysticism of small esteem—we will see that there are other forms of knowing which by their very structure are not communicable, and yet they continually cheer the prisoners of silence. My objection to mysticism is that out of the mystic vision no intellectual benefit redounds to mankind. Fortunately some mystics were thinkers of genius before they were mystics—men like Plotinus, Meister Eckhart, and Bergson. In these men the fertility of thought, logical or expressed, contrasts curiously with the poverty of what they discovered when in a state of ecstasy.

Mysticism tends to exploit the profound and to speculate on the characteristics of the abyss; at least it feels itself attracted by the depths and grows enthusiastic over them. The tendency of philosophy is precisely the opposite. It is not interested in submerging itself in the profound, as is mysticism; on the contrary, it desires to emerge from the depths to the surface. Contrary to what is usually assumed, philosophy is a gigantic effort at superficiality, that is to say, at bringing up to the surface and making open, clear, and evident that which was subterranean, mysterious, and latent. It detests mysticism and the melodramatic gestures of the mystagogue. It can say of itself what Goethe said—"I declare myself to be of those who aspire to make of the obscure the clear."

Philosophy is an enormous appetite for the transparent and a resolute will toward midday. Its basic proposal is to bring to the surface, to declare and describe the veiled and the hidden—philosophy in Greece began by calling itself *aletheia*, which means the process of bringing out of hiding, of revealing, of unveiling; in short, of making manifest. And making manifest is nothing but talking, *logos*. If mysticism is keeping silent, philosophizing is saying, discovering in the great nakedness and transparency of the word the very being of things—ontology. Compared to mysticism, philosophy would prefer to be the secret which is shouted aloud.

I remember some years ago having published the following: "I understand perfectly, and in part I share, the lack of sympathy which the churches have shown toward the mystics, as if they feared that their ecstatic adventures would bring religion a lessening of prestige. The ecstatic is, more or less, a frenetic. Therefore he compares himself to a man gone in drink. He lacks measure, and mental clarity. To man's relationship with God he imparts an orgiastic character which is repugnant to the grave serenity of the true priest. The fact is that, with a rare coincidence, the Confucian man felt a disdain for the Taoist mystic which is akin to that felt by the Catholic theologian for the nun who believes herself in rapt illumination. In every order the partisans of tumult will prefer the anarchy and inebriation of the mystics to the clear and ordered intelligence of the priests, that is to say, of the Church. I am sorry not to be able to follow them in this preference. A question of veracity keeps me away. And it is this, that any theology seems to me to bring us much more of God, more hints and notions about divinity than do all the ecstasies of all the mystics put together.

"Because in place of approaching the ecstatic skeptically we must, as I said, take him at his word, receive whatever of his transcendent immersions he brings us, and then see if what he presents to us is worth the trouble. And the truth is that after going with him on his sublime voyage, what he manages to communicate to us is a thing of little moment. I believe that the European soul is now finding itself near a new experience of God, approaching new discoveries about that which is the most important of all realities. But I doubt very much that an enrichment of our ideas about the divine will come by the underground paths of the mystics rather than by the luminous ways of discursive thought. Theology is my choice and not ecstasy." *

* *Estudios del Amor*, Chapter VII. [Translator's note]

I am glad to see the awakening of a new theological movement in Germany, in the work of Karl Barth, which emphasizes that theology is δεολέγειν—talking of God, not remaining silent about Him.

Having said this in so limited a way, I do not consider myself therefore bound to deprecate the work of the mystic *thinkers*. In other meanings and dimensions they are of abundant interest. Today, more than ever, we must learn many things from them, including their idea of ecstasy—not the same as ecstasy itself—which certainly does not lack significance. Another time we will see what kind of significance. What I maintain is that mystic philosophy is not what we are attempting in the name of philosophy. Its only initial limitation is that it wishes to be a theoretic knowledge, a system of concepts, and thereby of things said. Going back, as I shall do so many times, to search for a term of comparison in modern science, I will say that if physics contains the total of all that can be measured, philosophy is the whole of what can be said about the Universe.

6

Theory and Belief. Joviality. Intuitive Evidence. Data for the Problem of Philosophy.

PHILOSOPHY, then, is nothing but an activity which concerns theoretic knowledge, a theory of the Universe. And even when the word "Universe," opening panoramic vistas before us, adds to the severe word "theory" a certain life and gaiety, we must not forget that what we are going to create is not the Universe, as though we were momentarily Gods, but only its theory.

Philosophy, then, is not the Universe, it is not even that close trafficking with the Universe which we call living. We are not going to live things, but simply to theorize about them, to contemplate them. And to contemplate a thing implies maintaining oneself outside it, resolved to keep a chaste distance between it and ourselves. We are attempting a theory, or what is the same thing, a system of concepts about the Universe. No less, but also no more. To find those concepts which, when set in a certain order, allow us to say how much it seems to us there is, or what the Universe is. We are not attempting anything tremendous. Although philosophic problems, being fundamental, have about them something of pathos, philosophy itself is not pathetic. It is more like a pleasant exercise, a favorite occupation. It is simply a matter of marrying our concepts one with another, like pieces in a picture puzzle. I would rather put it this way than to recommend philosophy with qualifications full of solemnity. Like all great human undertakings, it has a certain sportive dimension, and out of this it keeps a clean humor and a rigorous care.

I am going to say another thing which may seem strange to you at the moment, but which I have been taught by long experience, something that has value not only for philosophy but for all the sciences, for everything which in the strict sense of the term is theoretic. It is this: when anyone approaches science for the first time, the best way of easing him into it and of making clear to him what he is undertaking would be to say, "do not seek to be convinced by what you are going to hear and what you are told to think; do not take this so seriously, but treat it like a game in which you are invited to observe the rules."

The state of mind produced by this far from solemn attitude is the best atmosphere in which to begin scientific study. The reason is very simple; to the tyro in science the phrases "being convinced" and "taking seriously" imply a state of mind which is so firm, so solid, so deep in itself that it can only make itself felt toward that which is most habitual and long-established. I mean to say that the kind of conviction with which we believe that the sun sets behind the horizon, or that bodies which we see are in fact outside ourselves, is so blind, so rooted in the habits by which we live and which form part of us, that an opposite conviction reached through astronomy or idealist philosophy can never compare with it in psychological brute force. A scientific conviction, for the very reason that it is founded on truths, on reasons, does not come, nor has it reason to come, from the skin of our souls. It has no spectral character. It is, in fact, a conviction out of pure intellectual assent which sees itself forced by specific reasons; it is not like faith and other vital beliefs that spring from the deepest root of our persons. Scientific conviction, when it is truly that, comes from without, δύραδεν, as Aristotle said, from the things to be grasped on the periphery of ourselves.

On that periphery is intelligence. Intelligence is not the deepest part of our being, but quite the contrary. It is like a sensitive skin, provided with tentacles, covering the rest of our innermost bulk, which in itself is, *senus stricto,* unintelligent and irrational. Barrès said it very well, "L'intelligence, quelle petite chose à la surface de nous." There it is, spread like a film over our innermost being, standing between things and the self—its role is not to be the self, but to reflect it, to mirror it. So much is it not us, that intelligence is the same thing in everybody, although some have a greater share of it than others. But whatever portion they have is the same kind of thing in all of them: two plus two equals four for everyone. Therefore Aristotle and the followers of Averroës believed that there was in the Universe a single *nous* or intellect, that insofar as we were intelligent, we were all one single intelligence.

What makes us individuals lies behind that. At the moment we are not going to delve into so difficult a question. What I have said is enough to suggest that intelligence will compete in vain against beliefs which are habitual and irrational. Whenever a scientist upholds his ideas with a faith like that of vital, living faith, doubt his science. In one of Baroja's books one character says to another, "This man believes in anarchy as in the Virgin of the Pillar"; whereupon a third comments, "Believing is believing, and always the same."

In a similar fashion, hunger and thirst for eating and drinking will always be psychologically stronger, will have a greater degree of psychic brute energy, than hunger and thirst for justice. The more elevated is an activity in an organism, the less vigorous it is, less stable and less efficient. The vegetative functions flag less quickly than do the sense functions, and the latter less than those that are voluntary and reflective. As the biologists say, the functions most recently acquired by a species, being higher and more complex, are those most easily lost. In other words, that which is most valued is always in greatest peril. In cases of conflict, of depression, of passion we are always quick to drop intelligence. It is as though we carried intelligence about us hung from a pin. Or to put it another way—he who is most intelligent is so— at times. And we could say the same thing of moral sense and esthetic taste. In man, by his very essence, the superior is always less effective than the inferior, less firm, less quick to impose himself. This idea would be useful in trying to understand universal history. In order to play his full part in history, the superior man must always wait till the inferior offers him place and occasion. The inferior is charged with the fulfillment of the superior— he lends him his strength, blind but incomparable.

Hence reason ought not to be proud, but should attend and minister to the less rational powers. The idea cannot fight face to face with instinct; it must insinuate itself bit by bit, must tame instinct, conquer it, enchant it, not like Hercules with his fists—it has no fists—but with supernal music, as Orpheus seduced wild beasts. The idea is—feminine and employs the immortal tactics of femininity, which does not seek to impose itself directly, as does man, but passively, almost atmospherically. Woman goes into action with a sweet appearance of absence of action, supporting, conceding; as Hebbel said, "In her, to do is to suffer"—*durch Leiden tun*. So is it with the idea. The Greeks suffered the basic error of believing that the idea, by virtue of being clear and only by this, imposed itself, fulfilled itself, that the *logos,* the word, was by itself and not otherwise made flesh. Outside of religion, this is a magical belief, and historical reality, for good or for bad, is not magic.

This is why I prefer that the curious approach philosophy without taking it very seriously, in the frame of mind which leads one to undertake a sport or occupy oneself with a game. Compared with life, a theory is not a grave, terrible, and formal thing, but a kind of play. "What I mean to say is that man is as a toy in the hands of God, and this ability to be a game is in truth the best there is in him. Therefore everyone, man or woman, contrary to the opinion which now rules, should aspire to this end and make of most beautiful games the true content of his life. Play, games, jests, culture, these we affirm are the most serious things in life for mankind."

Here is one more bit of frivolity which I cast on the breeze. But if I now pronounce it, it is not I who thought it, said it, or wrote it. The words I read to you are by no less a master than Plato. And they were not written casually, but a few paragraphs after having said that the theme on which he was going to talk was one of those which require the greatest tact when he who is about to speak has, as Plato had, reached old age. It is one of the few places in which Plato, always hidden behind his own text, throws open the luminous lines of his writing like a curtain of iridescent threads and allows us to see his own noble figure. Those words are from book VII of *The Laws*—Plato's last work, unfinished; his friend death surprised him leaning above it, lifting it forever in his immortal hand.

But there is still more. Plato says this after first announcing, with a rare insistence, that he is going to determine what is the state of mind, the temper, the emotional tone, we would say today, in which each life must take its stand as soon as it becomes mature. Although the Greeks were ignorant of most of what we call psychology (and we will see why), Plato out of his genius here foresaw one of the latest psychological discoveries, according to which our inner life springs, as from a seed, out of a fundamental emotional tonality which differs in every individual and which constitutes the basis of character. Every one of our concrete reactions is determined by that emotional base—melancholy in some, exalted in others, depression here, security there. Well then, in order to become cultivated and mature, man must provide himself with an adequate emotional tone which will be to his life what the keel laid by the carpenter is to the ship. Plato tells us that as he was writing this book he saw himself like that ship's carpenter on the river's edge —like that *naupegos*. The keel of culture, the state of mind which carries and balances it, is that serious jest, that formal jibe which resembles energetic play, resembles sport—understanding sport to mean an effort which, in contradistinction to work, is not imposed upon us, not utilitarian nor paid for, but a spontaneous, luxury effort that we make for the pleasure of making it, an effort that takes pleasure in itself. As Goethe said, "The song that the throat sings is the perfect prize for him who sings it."

Culture springs forth and lives, flowers and bears fruit, in a spiritual tone that is instinct with good humor—a kind of joviality. Seriousness will come later, when we have acquired culture or reached that form of it to which we are now attending—namely, philosophy. But for the moment the tone is joviality. This is not a state of mind which can be regarded as in any way contemptible; remember that joviality is no less than the state of mind in which Jove usually found himself. In training ourselves to joviality we do it in imitation of Olympic Jove.

And so Plato in his last works is pleased again and again to play with the two words which in Greek sound almost alike—παιδεία, culture, and παιδιά, child's play, jest, joviality. It is the irony of his master, Socrates, that flowers again in Plato's old age. And this irony produced the most ironic effects; in the codices where these last books of Plato have reached us, the copyist did not know when to write "paideia"—culture—and when to write "paidia" —a joke.[1] So one is invited to a hard game, for man is in the game where it is most rigorous. This jovial intellectual rigor is theory, and as I said, philosophy, a poor little thing, is no more than theory.

But also we know from Faust that "All theory, dear friend, is gray, and the golden tree of life is green." Gray is the ascetic aspect of color. Such is its symbolic value in ordinary language, and it is to this symbol that Goethe alludes. To be gray is the most that color can do when it desires to renounce its role as color; on the other hand, life is a green tree—which is an extravagant statement— and moreover that green tree of life turns out to be gilded, which is a still greater extravagance. This elegant wish to take refuge in gray when confronted with the marvelous and contradictory chromatic extravagance of life leads us to theorize. In theory we exchange reality for its ghost; this is what concepts are. Rather than living life we think about it. Yet who knows whether, under this

[1] Stenzel: *Der Begriff der Erleuchtung bei Platon,* Die Antike, II, 256.

apparent asceticism and withdrawal from life, which is what hard thinking is, there may not be hidden a maximum form of vitality, its supreme luxury! Who knows if thinking about life may not be a way of adding to the ingenuous process of living a magnificent eagerness for super-living!

Following the dramatic tactic of the mystics, I should tell you that we have now finished our second turn of the spiral and are about to enter on the third. But this new circle is of a very different quality from the two earlier ones. We have defined what we are attempting in the name of philosophy as one defines a project and a proposition. We have said that it is knowledge of the Universe, and that because of the limitless breadth and the problem-filled character of its theme, all philosophic thought must obey two laws, or obligations; first, it must be autonomous, admitting no truth which it does not itself construct, and second, it must obey the law of *pantonomy*, of not contenting itself with any position which does not express universal values; in short, which does not aspire to the Universe.

This is all that we have done in the last four chapters. Everything that I said was said only to clarify and give meaning to that minuscule doctrine. Therefore, as the other things of which I talked were not then important for themselves, we talked of them vaguely, almost as mere allusions. We thought of them as at a distance, indirectly, as things heard about. What I am trying to say is that the subjects of which we talked were not themselves present in our minds. We talked of this and that, but we did not bring those things before us so that we could see them directly, in their own body and being.

Well then, when one talks about something which is

not seen face to face one speaks more or less blindly and
without evidence. Now a theory is truly truth only when
it is made up of evidence and proceeds by means of evidence. A theory is made up of combinations, of concepts, of what we call judgments or propositions—of
phrases, if you wish. In these phrases we say that certain
things are of such and such a kind and no other. Well
then, a statement is true when we can confront what it
says with the very things of which it speaks. For the
moment, truth is the coincidence between talking about
a thing and the thing of which one talks. The thing itself
is present before us in vision: it may be in the form of
sentient vision, with the thing itself perceptible to the
senses, like colors and sounds, or it may be in a nonsen-
tient vision, where the thing is not a matter of the senses,
as, for example, our inner states of joy and sorrow; or
justice; or a geometric triangle, or goodness, relationships,
and so on.

A statement, then, is true in the measure in which the
things of which it speaks can be seen. And when we
accept the truth of a statement, taking our stand on the
fact that we are seeing the very thing which we understand by the meaning of the words we are hearing, that
statement is an evident truth. Evidence is not a sentiment
which incites us to tie ourselves to one phrase and not
to another. On the contrary, when it is sentiment and
only sentiment, feeling of whatever kind, that forces us
to accept a proposition as truth, that proposition is false.
Evidence has nothing to do with feeling; one could almost say that it is the opposite of sentiment, which by its
very nature is blind, not out of illness or accident, but
from birth. Joy or sorrow, enthusiasm or anguish, love
or hatred are blind because they have no eyes, as a plant
or a stone has no eyes. Where it is said that love is blind,

many foolish things are said along with it, but one of these rests on the fact that in that phrase love appears with a scarf across the eyes, like one who might see, but has been blinded. However, the peculiar thing about love is not the fact that it is blind, but that it has no eyes, nor ever has had.

Evidence, on the contrary, is the character which our judgments or our statements take on when the things that we assert in them are asserted because we have seen them. But we should not cling to the word "see," the word "vision," in the hope of finding in them a clarity and a precision which they do not possess. Of that we hold only this bit: we say that we see a color when the object called color is immediately before us, in person, so to speak. On the other hand, when we do not see a color but think about it, for example when we now think of the rosy color native to the sands of the Sahara, this color is not immediately present. Nothing of it is before us: the only thing we have is our thinking about it, directing ourselves toward it, referring ourselves to it mentally. What is important to us about vision is that in it we have the most obvious example of a subjective state in which objects are presented to us without any intermediary. We have another example of the same thing in hearing; the sound is, in the hearing of it, immediately present to us. In general, all the sense functions belong to this type of immediate presentation.

Positivism was right when it wished to reduce strict knowledge to what is present before us; its mistake was that it arbitrarily recognized no other immediate presence than that of objects perceptible to the senses—colors, sounds, odors, tactile qualities. Positivism was right insofar as it demanded the "positive," that is to say, the presence of the object itself, but it was not right when it reduced itself to the sensory. And even as sensism it was narrow; since its day a number of new senses have been discovered in man. The old Positivism was content with the five traditional senses. Our repertory has been so augmented that man now enjoys at least eleven senses.

But quite apart from this inadequicy we accuse Positivism of a vicious circle. Because it says, "Of nothing can we truthfully say that it exists if it is not present before us, and by present I understand being perceptible to the senses." Note that being perceptible to the senses and being present before us are two very different ideas. Color and sound are perceptible to the senses not because they are at times present before us, but because of their sensory condition as color and sound. On the other hand, justice and the triangle of pure geometry, even though present before us in person, could never be felt, never be perceived by the senses, for the very reason that they are not colors nor odors nor sounds. Positivism would have to demonstrate that there is no immediate presence but that of sensory objects, and then it would be right. But in order to do this it begins by affirming as a principle the very thing it would have to prove. Thus to commit a *petitio principii* it encloses itself in a vicious circle, a *circulus in demonstrando*.

Presence and sensifacience [2] are, I repeat, two ideas which have nothing to do with each other. The first speaks to us of a way in which objects stand before us, present and immediate, in contradistinction to other ways by which objects may stand in relation to our minds; for example, not presented to us, but represented, as the image of something which we have present before us

[2] Ortega's word is *sensualidad*, but its English equivalent refers only to the nature of man, not of objects that touch man's senses. [Translator's note]

is not the object itself, but a copy, a transcription, an image of it. On the other hand, the sensifacient is one class of objects as compared with another, objects that speak to the senses, and it does not concern the manner in which those objects appear in relation to us. And as it would be an obvious error to ask of us that we should, *sensu stricto,* see sounds or hear colors, it is a deeper error to deny the possible immediate presence of things that by their own nature are not perceptible to the senses. Descartes made it clear that no one had ever been able to see a polygon with a thousand sides, and yet there is no doubt that such a thing can be immediately present before us, as easily as the simple quadrangle. The proof of this is the fact that we understand the exact meaning of the phrase "a thousand-sided polygon" and we never confuse it with one that has more sides or with one that has less.

So one must keep the Positivist imperative of immediate presence, while at the same time saving it from its Positivist narrowness. Let us demand of every object that it be present before us so that we can speak of it with truth, but leave this presence to be adequate to the peculiarity of the object. This implies a radical broadening of Positivism, and as I wrote some years ago, modern philosophy might be characterized as "Absolute Positivism, in contradistinction to a partial and limited Positivism." And as we shall see, this absolute Positivism does correct and overcome the vice from which philosophy has always suffered more or less—overemphasis on the senses. Sometimes, as with almost all of the English, philosophy has been formally and consciously a matter of the senses. At other times it has wished not to be so, but it has dragged sensism along with it regardless, like a slave's chain, as in Plato himself, and even in Aristotle. Otherwise the problem of universals would not have been so enormous as it became for the Middle Ages. But let us leave this matter to itself.

What is now urgent is to insist that there is no truth which is strictly theoretic except that which is founded on evidence; this implies that in order to talk about things we must insist on seeing them, and by seeing them let us understand that they shall be immediately present before us, in the manner imposed by their composition. Hence in place of vision, which is a narrow term, we will talk of intuition. Intuition is of all things in the world the least magical and mystical: its precise meaning is that mental state in which an object is present before us. Therefore there will be intuition of that which concerns the senses, but also intuition of that which does not touch them.

There is an intuition of the color of an orange, of the orange itself, of the spherical figure of the orange. In all these cases, as whenever it is pronounced, the word *intuition* denotes immediate presence. Let us now compare the manner in which these objects—color, the orange, and the sphere—appear in our presence.

Before the luminous range of shades which the prism offers we can search with our eyes for the thing we think of when we hear the phrase "orange color." We find the color in our minds, and our eyes present us with that color; our thought of "orange color" finds itself intuitively fulfilled, realized, satisfied in the vision we then hold. As in thinking of this color we thought only of it, and then found before us the very thing of which we were thinking, without any addition or subtraction between the thought and the color, we can say that the concept and the thing seen were identical one with the other, or, which is the same thing, that we have a full and complete intuition of the color.

This is not what happens with the object called "an orange." What is it that we think of, or refer to mentally, when we think of an orange? Of a thing that has many attributes: in addition to its color it has a spherical figure which is solid, made up of matter that is more or less resistant. The orange of which we think has an outside and an inside; being a spherical solid, it will have two halves or hemispheres. Can we, in fact, see all of this? We very quickly realize that however we try, we can in each case see only half the orange, that half or hemisphere which faces us. By an inexorable visual law, the half of the orange which we have before our eyes will hide the other half which lies behind it. In a second act of vision, distinct from the first, we can turn it around and then see the other half. But then we will have to give up seeing the first hemisphere. The two of them never stand before our eyes together. Moreover, we see for the moment only the outside of the fruit; the inside remains hidden by the surface. We can cut the orange into slices and then, by new visual acts, see its interior, but those slices will never be so thin as to let us say that in fact we have seen the whole of the orange, exactly as we thought of it.

Hence there is every evidence that we are wrong when we say that we see an orange. Never do we find present before us, either in one single vision or in many partial visions, the whole of it as our thought presents it to us. We always think of more of it than we have present before us; our concept of it always presupposes something which vision does not give us. This means that of the orange, as of all corporeal things, we have only an incomplete or inadequate intuition. Moment by moment we can add a new vision of a thing to what we have already seen of it—we can cut a thinner piece of orange, and thus make visible something that was previously hidden—but this shows only that our intuition of bodies, of material things, though it can be indefinitely perfected, will never reach the point of totality and completeness. That intuition which is incomplete, but always susceptible of being indefinitely moved toward perfection, always coming closer and closer to being complete, we call "experience." Of material things we can only have knowledge by experience, that is, knowledge which is merely approximate, but always susceptible of closer approximation.

The color called orange was not a body, not a material thing. It was color only, pure and alone, separate and apart from the thing which carries it, from the material that gives it physical existence. Because it was no more than an abstract object we were able to see it complete.

Let us now address ourselves to the third object under consideration: the circle described in geometry. We find at once that none of the circles materially existent, or which we could construct, the circles drawn on the blackboards of polytechnic schools and in books of geometry, none of these circles conform strictly and exactly to our concept of a circle. Therefore the object, "circle," is not visible in a sense form, not visible to the eyes in one's head. Yet it is indubitably present before us.

But if we did not obtain the idea of a circle from the circles we see, where did it come from? Concepts are not invented, they are not plucked out of nothingness. The concept, the idea, is always an idea of something, and that something must somehow have been present before us in order that we may afterwards think it. Even though we had the power of creating *ex nihilo*, out of nothing, we would first have to create the object, then have it present before us and then think it. Of the circle we have an immediate intuition; we can always find it in our minds without any need for an image, which at best would be only an approximation; and we can compare our concept of the circle with the circle itself.

To analyze what makes up that pure and extrasensory intuition of objects would take too long, but the following explanation will clear the matter. The circle is, in the first place, a line; by "line" we understand an infinite series of points. However short and finite the line may be, the thing we think of as a line is that infinite joining of points. Well now, what does one mean by that phrase "infinite points"? When we think of that concept, how many points do we think of? "An infinite number." Pardon me, but what we are asking is whether, if on thinking of "the infinite" in the matter of points, we are thinking of each and every one and all of the points that make up that infinite. Certainly not. We think only of a finite number of them, and to this we add that we could always think of one point more, and another, and another, without ever coming to an end.

The result is that in thinking of an infinite number we think that we can never stop thinking, that the concept of the infinite implies the recognition that this does not contain all that is meant; or, which is the same thing, that the object of which we are thinking—the infinite— exceeds our concept of it. But this suggests that in thinking of the infinite, we are constantly comparing our concept with the infinite itself, therefore with its presence, and that on making this comparison we find our concept falling short. In the case of an intuition of a mathematical continuum, such as the line, we see that intuition does not coincide with the concept; but unlike the case of the orange, intuition here gives more rather than less than what was in the thought. And in fact, an intuition of the continuum, of what we call, and think of, as infinite, cannot be reduced to the concept, to *logos* or *ratio*. That is to say, the continuum is irrational, beyond the conceptual, or meta-logical.

The rationalism of recent times has wanted to create for itself illusions (rationalism is in essence a proud living on illusion) out of which it could reduce the mathematical infinite to a concept, a *logos;* with Cantor it broadened (*soi-disant* by pure logic) the mathematical sciences, extending their field prodigiously in a rude and imperialist fashion which was very like the nineteenth century. The broadening process was achieved by dint of blindness toward the problem itself, and it was necessary to give free rein to certain basic and insoluble contradictions—the famous "antinomy of the groups" so that mathematicians could come back to sanity, and the supposed mathematical logic return to intuition. This movement, which is of incalculable importance, is taking place at the present time. The new mathematics recognizes the fragment of irrationality which exists in its object—that is to say, it accepts its own destiny, leaving to logic the same privilege.

So we are left with the fact that mathematical objects, including the most strange and mysterious of them, the continuum, are immediately present before us; we find them either in an adequate intuition just as we think them, or with an even richer content than we think. But where there is the most there is also the least. In order to recognize, with evidence, the truth of our propositions, it is for the moment enough that all which is thought in them should be found in intuition. The fact that this intuition may also contain other elements that we neither could think nor wanted to think does not affect the primary meaning of the truth. Strictly speaking, intuition always contains more than we think. Thus, in the simplest of the three cases analyzed, the case of the color called "orange," the color as seen will always have a tint which our concept does not determine, which we can neither think nor name. And this is because the color called orange, being somewhere between red and yellow, presents a variety of orange tones that are literally infinite. The spectrum, too, is a continuum, although qualitative rather than mathematical.

Well then, of everything brought before us through an adequate intuition, we can speak with strict (and not merely approximate) truth; that is to say, we have close knowledge of it, knowledge that is once and forever valid. This is what is called in philosophy by the venerable but absurd and even ugly name of knowledge a priori. In this sense, mathematics is knowledge a priori, and neither experimental nor empirical as is our knowledge of the orange. As this latter never surrenders wholly to vision, but always holds within itself something still to be seen, our knowledge of it must depend on what can be seen even while recognizing that this is not definitive. It is knowledge circumscribed by each new vision, ascribed to the relativity of each observation which is made a posteriori.

The triangle, on the other hand, however we wish to think of it, offers itself to us whole and complete. There it is, hiding nothing of its shape, its content or its composition, exemplary in its nakedness, present to its very backbone. Our thought can take centuries in thinking out all the theorems which can be extracted from a single intuition of the triangle; in the process we must renew that intuition again and again, but the last flash of intuition will add nothing to the first.

The fundamentalism of philosophy will not permit it

to accept for its own phrases any other mode of truth than that of total evidence founded on adequate intuition. This is why it was inexcusable to dedicate most of this chapter to the theme of intuitive evidence, which is the basis of the philosophy most characteristic of our time. I do not think it would be possible to reduce so bitter a question to smaller compass. But the difficult draught is down and I now hope—I am not sure, but I hope—that the rest of the course may seem a smooth and comfortable descent into subjects which are warmer and nearer to our hearts. It was essential to interpolate those suggestions about evidence, for, as I said earlier, the new circle on which we are now about to enter differs from the earlier ones in that we will now be talking of things which oblige us to see them while we meditate about them. Hence if, up to now, we have made only a kind of preparation for entering into philosophy—like the disconnected sounds which instruments emit while being tuned before the real music begins—we are now ready for philosophy.

As we again pass on our spiral track the point that marks our start, let us sound once again like a *leitmotiv* the definition of philosophy. Let us repeat it. Philosophy is knowledge of the Universe, of all that there is. By now I assume that these words echo with their full charge of intellectual electricity, in all their breadth and all their dramatic intensity. (We already know the deep-rooted character of our problem and of the demands which this imposes on our type of philosophic truth. The first of these was not to accept as true anything which we ourselves had not tested and proved, nothing whose basis of truth we ourselves had not constructed. Therefore our most habitual and plausible beliefs, those which constitute the assumptions, the native soil on which we live, remain in suspension. In this sense philosophy is anti-natural, and as I said, paradoxical to its very root. The "*doxa*" is opinion which is daily and spontaneous; even more, it is "natural" opinion. Philosophy sees itself obliged to give this up, to go above or below it in search of another opinion, another *doxa* which is firmer than that which is spontaneous. This, then, is the *para-doxa*.)

If our problem is to know whatever there is, to know the Universe, the first thing we must do is to determine what things there are, out of those there may be, of which we can be sure that they exist. Perhaps there are, in the Universe, many things of whose existence we are ignorant and will always be ignorant, or vice-versa; many others that we believe to be in the Universe, but are wrong about; that is to say, they are not truly in the Universe but only in our beliefs—they are illusions. The thirsty caravan believes it sees in the desert distance a wavy line where the freshness of water trembles under the sun. But this beneficent water is not out there in the desert, it exists only in the imagination of the caravan.

One must therefore distinguish these three classes of things: those which may exist in the Universe, whether we know it or not; those which we mistakenly think are there, but which in truth are not; and finally, those of which we can be sure that they are there. These last will be the ones that are both in the Universe and within our knowledge. They will be what we undoubtedly have of what there is, that part of the Universe which is given to us beyond question—in short, the data of the Universe.

Every problem assumes the existence of data. The data are what is not a problem. In the traditional example which we repeated the other day—that of the stick submerged in the water—the impression given by touch, which shows us the stick quite straight, is datum, and so is that given by vision, which shows us the stick as broken. The problem emerges in the measure in which those two conflicting bits of evidence constitute not a problem, but a pair of effective and indisputable facts. Then their contradictory character rises before us, and it is this of which every problem consists. The facts give us a partial and insufficient reality; they present us with something which, on the other hand, I hope could not be, something that contradicts itself. A reality in which a stick is at once and the same time straight and broken. The more clear and evident this is, the more unacceptable it becomes, the more a problem, the more a non-being.

So that thought may act, there must be a problem before it, and in order that there may be a problem there must be data. Unless something is given us it does not occur to us to think of it or about it; and if everything were given us we would have no reason to think. The problem supposes an intermediate situation: that something is given, and that what is given is incomplete, is in itself not enough. If we did not know a thing we would not know that it is incomplete, defective, that we lack certain other things which are postulated by the thing we already have. This is the consciousness of a problem. It is the knowing that we do not know enough, it is knowing that we are ignorant. And such, strictly speaking, was the deep meaning of "knowing that he did not know" which Socrates attributed to himself as his only pride. Not surprising, for the consciousness of problems is the beginning of science.

Hence Plato asked, "What being is capable of cognitive activity?" Not the animal, for it is ignorant of everything, including its own ignorance, and nothing can move it to emerge from that. But neither is it God, who knows everything in advance and has no reason to make any effort. Only an intermediate being, somewhere between God and the animal, dowered with ignorance but at the same time aware of this ignorance, feels himself impelled to emerge from it and goes, tense and eager, in one dynamic burst, from ignorance to knowledge. This intermediate being is man. It is the specific glory of man to know that he does not know—this makes him the divine beast weighted with problems.

As our own problem is the Universe, or all that there is, we must determine what facts about the Universe we have, or to put it another way, what, among all there is, has so surely been given to us that we need not search for it. What we do need to search for will be what we lack because it is not given us.

But what are the data in philosophy? The other sciences, whose type of truth is less basic, are also less basic in the stability, the firmness, of their data. But in this first step philosophy must carry its intellectual heroism to an extreme, and its strictness to a superlative degree. This is why, although the data themselves are not a problem, there rises on the threshold of philosophy the enormous and intolerable problem of what data there are for the Universe, the problem of what there surely and indubitably is.

7

Facts of the Universe. The Cartesian Doubt. Theoretic Primacy of the Conscious. The Self as Gerfalcon.

As I was saying, it is very important for us to distinguish between three classes of things: those which may be in the Universe, whether or not we know it; those which we mistakenly believe to be there, but which in truth are not; and, finally, those which we can be sure are there. These last are the ones which are both in the Universe and within our knowledge.

But in this last class we still must establish a new division. Our sense of certainty with respect to the existence of an object in the Universe is of two types: sometimes we assert the existence of an object on the basis of reasoning, with proof, or with a firm and justified inference—thus when we see smoke we infer that there is fire, although we do not see the fire; when we see certain lineal forms in the trunk of a tree we infer that something has been there, perhaps a man, or that mysterious insect which, marching across the tree, has left inscribed there figures similar to printed letters—it is therefore called *"bastrichus typographus."*

This certainly by inference, proof or reasoning, affirms

the existence of certain objects by starting from another and earlier certainty about another object. Thus to affirm the existence of fire implies that we have seen smoke. Therefore, in order to affirm the existence of certain objects by means of inference or proof one must start with a more basic and primary certainty in the existence of other objects; a type of certainty which needs neither proof nor inference. There are, then, things whose existence we can and must prove—but this assumes that there are things whose existence we neither can nor need to prove, because they prove themselves. One can only prove what one can sensibly doubt—but that which does not tolerate doubt neither needs nor permits of proof.

These things whose existence is indubitable, which reject all possible doubt, which deprive it of meaning and destroy it, these things which are proof against everything including a bombardment of criticism, are the data of the Universe. I repeat, then, data are not the only things there are in the Universe, nor even the only things which are surely there, but they are the only things which there are without any slightest doubt, things whose existence is based on a most special certainty, an indubitable certainty, an arch-certainty.

These data of the Universe we are now going to search out.

I remember having read years ago in the verses of a contemporary poet and compatriot, Juan Ramón Jiménez:

> The garden has a fountain
> And the fountain a chimera
> And the chimera a mistress
> Who is dying of sorrow.

From whence it appears that in the world where *there are* gardens *there are* also chimeras and these are capable

of leading a poet to write of death. If such things are
not there, how is it that we talk of them and distinguish
them from other beings, that we define their shape and
even paint them and model them for the plashing foun-
tains of our gardens? And as the chimera is only the
representative of a whole related fauna, we might say
that there are also centaurs and tritons, griffins, unicorns,
a pegasus and passionate minotaurs. But shortly—perhaps
too shortly—we solve the question of the chimera by saying that we are talking about a phantasmagoric assemblage
which exists not in the Universe, but solely in fancy or
imagination. Thus we take the chimera out of the real
garden where it pretends to live with the swans and to
flirt with the poets, and we put it inside a mind, a soul, a
psyche. In doing this we feel that we have found the
proper place for the difficult burden of the chimera and
its too numerous fellows.

We take this resolution so promptly because in point
of fact the existence of the chimera offers doubts that
are so obvious, a reality so little probable that its case is
not worth major meditation—even though we are left
with an obscure sting in the depths of the soul, a sting
which, having been mentioned, I will erase from your
minds lest it disturb us or have any serious effect on our
discussion. The sting recalls a proposal of mine made
years ago in defense of Don Quixote. So we laugh because Don Quixote takes windmills to be giants! So Don
Quixote ought not to see a giant where he was really
seeing a windmill! But, why should man know anything
about giants? Where are there giants, where have there
been giants? But if there are none, or have been none,
man, the human species, must at some moment in its
history have discovered a giant where there was none—
at that moment it was man himself who was Don Quixote.

And in fact, the Universe for thousands of years seemed to man to be composed of giants and chimeras; these were the realest things that existed, these were what governed his life.

How was, how is, this possible? Here is the sting, the winged query which I left floating in the breeze of curiosity—but which, I repeat, does not affect our question. Another sting will have to be added to this, but this too we can quiet; for now we are not discussing whether there are or can be chimeras; what interests us is whether they exist beyond the shadow of a doubt, and as there is no difficulty whatever in doubting that they exist, they do not serve us as basic data concerning the Universe.

That physics assures us that there are in the Universe forces, atoms, electrons, is more serious. Are they there in fact, and without doubt? We hear the physicists disputing their existence among themselves; this indicates that it can at least be doubted. But even though the physicists should come to agreement, and in a united phalanx wish to make us believe in the real existence of forces we do not see, of invisible atoms and electrons, we would offer in opposition the following reflection: atoms are objects whose existence, effective though it may be, appears to us only at the end of a whole theory. For the existence of atoms to be true, the entire physical theory must first be true. And the physical theory, true though it may be, is a problematical truth which consists in and is founded on a long series of reasonings. This, then, implies the need to prove them. Therefore the physical theory is not a primary, self-evident truth, but, in the best light that can be put on it, is a truth which is derived and inferred. This leads us to say of it something akin to what we said of the chimera which exists solely in the imagination; namely, that it is doubtful that there really are atoms; for the moment, they exist solely in theory, in the thinking of physicists. At present, atoms are the chimeras of physics, and just as the poets imagine the chimera to have claws, so Lord Kelvin attributed to atoms a set of hooks and crooks.

No more than chimeras are atoms indubitable; they are not data of the Universe.

Therefore let us search among things that are nearer us, and less problematical. The results of all the natural sciences may well be questionable, but at least the things that surround us, things that we see and touch, which the sciences examine as effective facts, will possess an existence which cannot be suspected. Even though the poet's chimera does not exist, the garden undoubtedly does, the real garden, visible, tangible, smellable, which can be bought and sold, pruned and walked in.

Yet when I am in the garden enjoying its new spring-time green it occurs to me to close my eyes: as if I had touched a magic switch the garden vanishes—in one moment it is annihilated, blotted out of the Universe. Our eyelids, closing like the guillotine's knife, cut it from the world. Nothing of it remains, not a grain of earth, not a petal, nor the indentation of a leaf. But if I open my eyes again, the garden with no less speed comes back into being; like a transcendent dancer, it springs in a leap from non-being into being, and bearing no trace of its momentary death, sets itself courteously before me. The same thing happens with its fragrances, or its tactile qualities, if I manipulate the corresponding senses.

But there is even more to this; resting in the garden I fall asleep, and sleeping, I dream that I am in the garden, and while I am dreaming, the dreamed-of garden seems to me no less real than the one I saw. In Hebraic-Egyptian, *garden* means *paradise*. If I drink certain alcoholic beverages, I also contrive, even though awake, to see gardens like that. These are the gardens of hallucination, the artificial paradises. *In itself* the garden of hallucination differs from the authentic garden not at all; that is to say, both of them are equally authentic. Perhaps everything that surrounds me, the whole external world in which I live, is only one vast hallucination. At least, its perceptible content is the same in normal perception as in hallucination. Well, now, the characteristic thing about hallucination is that its object has no existence in reality. Who will assure me that this is not also true of normal perception? This differs from hallucination only in that it is more constant and its content is as relatively common to other men as to me. But this does not allow us to take away from normal perception its possibly hallucinatory character; we can only say that perception of the real is in fact not just any hallucination but a constant and communal hallucination—that is to say, much worse than the other.

So it is that the so-called facts of the senses fail to give us anything authentic, anything which in itself guarantees its existence. According to this argument, life will be a correct and monotonous dream, a hallucination which is daily and tenacious.

Doubt, methodic doubt, dropping like nitric acid, has corroded and volatilized the solidity, the security of the external world; or, to use another image, like the undertow at low tide, doubt has carried out and drowned in non-being the entire world around us, with all its things and all its people, including our own bodies, which we touch in vain to assure ourselves that they indubitably exist, in order to save them; doubt floods across the world, and there we see that world underneath the cur-

rent, wrecked and extinguished. Of him who dies, the
Chinese say that he has "gone down to the river."

You will surely note the full gravity of the result
which has been imposed on us. What has been said means
no less than that things, nature, other human beings, the
whole external world, have no evident existence, are not
a basic fact, are not something which there undoubtedly
is within the Universe. This world which surrounds us,
which carries and sustains us, seeming to us the most firm,
secure and solid thing, this *terra firma* on which we stamp
by way of asserting that it is the most immovable thing we
know—this takes on a dubious existence, or at least one
that can be suspected. And therefore philosophy cannot
use as its point of departure the fact of the existence of
the outside world—which is where our own belief begins. In life, we accept the full reality of our cosmic scene
with no shadow of a doubt, but philosophy, which cannot accept as truth a thing that another science demon-
strates to be true, can even less readily accept what life
believes.

Here is a concrete and superlative example of the way
in which the meaning of philosophizing is nonliving, a
tremendous demonstration of the reason why philosophy
is by nature paradoxical. To philosophize is not to live, it
is to stand consciously aside from vital beliefs. Well then,
this standing aside can not be, nor must it be, more than
virtual, intellective, executed for the exclusive purpose of
creating theory; it is itself theoretic.

In short, this is why it seems to me grotesque to invite
people seriously to enter into philosophy. Who can pretend that any one "would be convinced," "would take
seriously" the assertion that the outside world does not
exist? Philosophic conviction is not vital conviction—
it is a quasi-conviction, a conviction of the intellect.

And to the philosopher seriousness does not mean solemnity, but merely the virtue of putting our concepts in series, in order.

But by all means note the following: philosophy begins by saying that the outside world is not a basic fact, that its existence can be doubted and that every proposition in which the reality of the outside world is affirmed is not an evident proposition but one which needs to be proved; in the best of cases it requires other primary truths on which to lean. What philosophy does *not* do, I repeat, is to deny the reality of the outside world, because that too would be to begin with something questionable. Strictly speaking, what philosophy says is only this: neither the existence nor the nonexistence of the world about us is certain, therefore one can start neither from the one or the other because that would mean starting from a supposition; and one is bound to start not from what is supposed, but from what one poses for oneself, that is to say, from what is imposed.

But let us go back to that dramatic situation in which the low tide of doubt with its strong undertow carried away the world and our friends, and with them our very bodies.

What, then, remains in the Universe? What is there in the Universe beyond any shadow of a doubt? When one has doubts about the world, and even about the entire Universe, what is left? The doubt is left, and the fact that I doubt; if I doubt that the world exists I cannot doubt that I doubt—here is the limit of all possible doubting. However broad we may leave the sphere of doubt we find that it stumbles over itself and is destroyed. Is it something indubitable that one seeks? Here it is— doubt. In order to doubt everything I must not doubt that I doubt. Doubt is only possible in exchange for not touching doubt; if it bites itself it will break its own tooth.

With this thought, which is only the *mise en scène* for another and much greater idea, Descartes begins modern philosophy. No one ignores this; it is an elemental bit of information. If I repeat it, along with other things which also *seemed* widely known and yet appeared in the first half of this course, it is for many reasons which may be mentioned later. We have reached a height at which the secrets of this course can be declared and their underground passages visited. So I now say what I have refrained from saying publicly for many years, and this is that to me the work of a publicist, or in general the life of a man in the fullness of its meaning, is like the Opera House in Paris, which has hidden below ground the same number of stories that it displays above the earth's surface. That I say this in passing, bowing before the colossal figure of Descartes, father of modernity, is, as we will see later, no accident.

But let us get on with more urgent matters.

Whoever thinks that Descartes inaugurated the modern age by producing that trifle about not doubting that we doubt (an idea which also occurred to St. Augustine) has not the least suspicion of the enormous innovation which Cartesian thought represents, and in consequence fails to understand the whole of what modernity has meant.

It is highly important that we see with the utmost clarity how privileged is the fact of doubt so that we may have no doubts about it; we must know why it is that we can doubt a thing as gigantic as the whole external world, while on the other hand the dart of doubt is blunted when it comes to this trifling business of doubt itself. When I doubt, I cannot doubt the existence of my doubt; this, then, is a basic fact, an unquestionable reality of the Universe. But why? That this theatre in which I am speaking really exists—this I can doubt, perhaps I am now living amid a hallucination. Perhaps, in my all-powerful youth, I once dreamed that I was talking of philosophy to a Madrid public in a theatre, and now I do not know whether that dream has come true this moment, or whether this moment is that dream and I am now that dreamer. What more could I wish! In content, the real world and the dream world are not basically different; they are adjacent compartments, separated only as Virgil's garden was said in the Middle Ages to be separated from the rest of the world, by a wall of air. We can move from the real world to the dream world without change, and in this specific example there is no doubt that to persuade the people of Madrid to concern themselves a bit with philosophy has been and still is the dream of my life.

So I can doubt the reality of this theatre, but not the fact that I doubt it; once more I repeat, why? The answer is that to doubt means that it *seems to me* that something is doubtful and problematical. For something to seem to me, and to think it, these are one and the same thing. Doubt is no more and no less than a thought. Now then, in order to doubt the existence of a thought I must perforce think this thought, must give it existence in the Universe, so that with the same act in which I try to suppress my thought I give it reality. Or, to put it another way, thought is the only thing in the Universe whose existence cannot be denied, because to deny is to think. The things of which I think may not exist in the Universe, but the fact that I think of them is indubitable.

Let me repeat: for something to be doubtful, it must *seem to me* that it is; and the entire Universe may *seem to me* doubtful, except for that fact of its *seeming to me*.

The existence of this theatre is problematical, for I understand its existence to mean that it may be what it pretends to be quite independently of me—that when I close my eyes and it ceases to have any existence for me, it goes on existing on its own account, outside of me and apart from me, in the Universe; that is to say, it would have a being *in itself*. But thought has the mysterious privilege that its being, the essence of what it pretends to be, is reduced to a *"seeming to me,"* a being *for* me. And as for the moment I consist only of my thought, we will say that thought is the only thing whose being, whose reality lies only in what it is to itself. It is what it seems to be, and nothing more; it seems to be what it is. It exhausts its essence in its appearance.

With respect to the theatre the situation is the opposite: what the theatre is or pretends to be is not exhausted with the fact of its appearing to me when I see it. On the contrary, it also pretends to exist when I do not see it, when it does not appear to me, when it is not present before me. But my seeing it is something which exhausts its existential pretense in the act of seeming to me that I am seeing; my seeing is present to me, patent and immediate. If I now am suffering a hallucination, this theatre will not really be existing, but the vision of this theatre is something which no one can ever take away from me.

From this reasoning comes the understanding that to thought is given only that part of the Universe which is thought itself. And it is given to thought because it consists only in the fact of being given, because it is pure presence, pure appearance, a pure "seeming to me." This is the magnificent, the decisive discovery of Descartes which, like a great wall of China, divides the history of philosophy into two great halves: the ancients and the men of the medieval world are on one side, the whole of modernity on the other.

But what I have said by no means satisfies me. As you see, I have been discussing a statement of capital importance, the theoretic primacy of the mind, of the spirit, the conscience, the "I," of the subjective as a universal fact; this is the primary fact of the Universe. Now then, to come upon this and consider it is the greatest idea that the modern age adds to the treasure come down from Greece. It is therefore important that we insist on this and that we aim for the maximum clarity concerning it. One must carry clarity almost to the point of madness, the madness of clarity. Therefore you will pardon me if I return again and again to the matter, seeking for different formulas so that all of you—some one way, some another—may enter into complete comprehension of what the mind is, what is the conscious state, thought, subjectivity, the spirit, the "I."

We were seeking the basic data of the Universe. But to what, to whom are these facts given? To knowledge, naturally. They are the facts for a knowledge of the Universe, that body of data of which knowledge must take charge in order to use it as a point of departure in the hunt for what may be lacking. And when can we say that something is given to knowledge? Obviously, when this something enters fully into our knowledge, when we find it clear and sure within our comprehension, without mystery and without doubt, when our knowledge possesses it without question. Well now, in order that I may enter into knowledgeable possession of something it is necessary that this something shall be made manifest to me, that it presents itself to me in its entirety, just as it is, as it pretends to be, with no part of its composition remaining hidden.

It is obvious that anything which pretends to exist, but is not present before me, is not data. But this happens with everything that is not my own thought, my own mind. For something to be present before me I must have it in some fashion within me, must think it. Everything which is apart from my thought pretends *ipso facto* to exist outside my thought—that it so say, apart from my presence. I do not stand witness for it. But thought, being only the things I have present before me insofar as they are present, things seen insofar as they are seen, things heard insofar as they are heard, things imagined insofar as they are imagined, that which takes the form of idea insofar as it does—thought holds fast to itself, is in complete possession of itself. If I think that two times two is equal to five, I think something that is false, but the fact that I think it is not false.

Thought, *cogitatio*, is the basic datum, because thought always holds fast to itself, it is the only thing which is present to itself and which consists in this finding of itself within itself. Now we see why the sting of doubt is only a sting, a sharp, conceptual, and prickly formula for a much broader idea. Not for any special factor of doubt within itself is doubt to be beyond doubting, but because it is one of so many thoughts or cogitations. The same thing we say about doubting we can say about our seeing and hearing, imagining, conceiving of ideas, feeling, loving, hating, wishing or not wishing, having a toothache. All these things have in common the fact they are whatever they may be to themselves. If it *seems* to me that my teeth ache, it is beyond question true that the fact called "toothache" exists in the Universe, for it is enough that it exists for itself, that it seems to itself to exist. Whether or not there are teeth in the Universe is still questionable; this is why the poet Heine told a lady that when we complain, although the woes themselves are most certain, we sometimes confuse the origin of our woes—"Madam, I tell you that I have a toothache in my heart."

Long years of teaching experience have taught me that it is very difficult for our Mediterranean peoples—and this is not chance—to recognize the peculiar character, unique among all the other things in the Universe, which constitutes thought and subjectivity. On the other hand, to the men of the north this is relatively easy and obvious. And as the idea of subjectivity is, as I have already said, the basic principle of the entire modern era, I leave with you in passing the hint that their failure to understand this is one of the reasons why the Mediterranean peoples have never become completely modern. Each era is like a climate where certain inspiring and organizing principles of life predominate; when this climate does not suit a people they lose interest in life, as a plant in an adverse atmosphere is reduced to a *vita minima*, or in sporting terms, it "loses form." This has been happening to the Spanish people during the so-called modern age. The modern type of life is one which does not interest them, does not suit them. There is no way of fighting against it; the only thing to do is to wait until it passes.

But suppose that this idea of subjectivity which is the root of modernity should be superseded, suppose it should be invalidated in whole or in part by another idea, deeper and firmer. This would mean that a new climate, a new era, was beginning. And as this new era means the contradiction of the previous era, of modernity, the peoples who have felt themselves battered by modern times would in all probability find themselves resurgent in the new period. Perhaps Spain would come fully awake again to life and to history. What if one of the results of this course should be to convince us that such an imagined thing has already become a fact, that the idea of subjectivity has given way before another idea, that modernity is basically finished?

But the idea of subjectivity, of the primacy of the mind, of consciousness as a primary fact of the Universe is so enormous, so firm, so solid, that we cannot create for ourselves an illusion that it will be easily overthrown; on the contrary, we must set ourselves within it, understand it and completely dominate it. Otherwise we could not even try to overcome it. Throughout history all conquest implies assimilation; we must devour what is going to be overcome, must take within ourselves the very thing we wish to abandon. In the life of the spirit only that is superseded which is conserved—as the third step rises higher than the first two because it has them beneath it. If they should disappear, the third step would fall back to being only the first. There is no other way of being more than modern than to have been profoundly modern. For this reason the Spanish ecclesiastical seminarians have never been able to advance beyond modern ideas—because they have never really wanted to accept them, but have stubbornly and continually stayed outside of those ideas, neither directing them nor assimilating them. In contrast to the life of the body, in the life of the spirit it is the new ideas, the daughter ideas, which carry their own mothers in their wombs.

But let us go back to the basic datum, which is thought.

Methodical doubt, the decision to doubt as long as doubt has an intelligible meaning, was for Descartes not a chance occurrence like his initial formula on the indubitability of doubt. The resolution of universal doubt is only the obverse or instrument of another and more positive resolution: that of not admitting as the content of a science anything that we cannot prove. Well, now, science, theory, is only the transcript of reality in a system of proven propositions. Methodic doubt is not an adventure in philosophy, it is philosophy itself, acting out of its own native condition. Every proof is proof of resistance—and theory is proof, proof of the resistance which a proposition offers to doubt. Without doubting there is no proving, no knowing.

This methodical doubt carried with it historically, as it carries for us today, the enormous reward that for knowledge there is no other basic fact than thought itself. Of no other single thing is it enough to say that in order for it to exist I have only to think it. The chimera and the centaur do not exist *because* I amuse myself by imagining them—as this theatre does not exist *because* I see it. On the other hand, it is enough that I think I am thinking this or that for this thinking to exist. So thinking has as its especial privilege the capacity to give being to itself, to become a fact for itself; or to put it another way, in all other things the fact that they exist and that I think about them are two different things—therefore they are always problem and not fact. But in order that a thought of mine shall exist it is enough that I think I am thinking it. Here, thinking and existing are one and the same thing. The reality of thinking consists of nothing more than the fact that I recognize I am thinking. Being consists in this recognition, in knowing itself. The basic fact in knowing would be that it consists in knowing itself, and in nothing else.

The kind of certainty with which we can affirm that thought or *cogitatio* exists in the Universe has a quality which cannot be compared with that of any other affirmation concerning existences; once we discover it, we must found upon it all our knowledge of the Universe.

For theory, the first truth about reality is this—thought exists, *cogitatio est*. We cannot take as our point of departure the reality of the outside world: everything that surrounds us, all bodies including our own, are suspect in their pretension that they exist in themselves and independently of our thinking of them. But on the other hand, it cannot be doubted that all this exists in my thought, as my ideas, as *cogitationes*. The result is that the mind becomes the center and support of all reality. My mind dowers whatever it thinks with an indestructible reality if I take that thinking for what it originally is —if I take it as my idea. This principle leads one to attempt a system of explanation of what there is, interpreting all that appears to be neither thought nor idea as consisting merely in having been thought, in being idea. This system is idealism, and modern philosophy since Descartes has been idealist at root.

If, a little while ago, in doubting the independent existence of the outside world we were calling it an enormous paradox, the immediate consequence of this doubt which converts that outside world into a mere thought of mine, will be the arch-paradox that makes of modern philosophy a conscious contradiction of our vital belief. Since the days of Descartes, philosophy has been moving in a direction which is opposite to our mental habits, moving upstream and against the life current, leaving that current at an accelerated pace until it reaches the point at which —in Leibnitz, Kant, Fichte or Hegel—philosophy becomes the world seen in reverse, a magnificent, antinatural doctrine of the initiate, a secret wisdom, an esoteric creed. Thought has swallowed up the world: things have turned into mere ideas.

In the passage to which I referred earlier, Heine asks his friend, "Madam, have you any idea of what an idea is? Because I asked my coachman yesterday what ideas were and he answered me, 'Ideas . . . Ideas, why ideas are the things which are put into one's head.' " For three centuries—the entire modern age—the splendid baroque coach which is idealist philosophy has been driven by Heine's coachman. Our prevailing culture still travels in that vehicle and no way has been found of getting out of it with intellectual honesty. Those who have tried this have not stepped out of it: they have simply thrown themselves through the little window and broken their heads—that head of Heine's coachman where things had been put.

The superiority of idealism comes from having discovered a thing whose manner of being is fundamentally different from that of all other things. No other thing in the Universe, even assuming that there might be other things, consists basically in being for its own sake, in recognition of itself. Neither colors, nor bodies, nor atoms, hence nothing material—the being of a color is to be white, to be green, to be blue, but not to be white or green or blue for itself. A body is gravity, weight, but not itself a matter of weighing. Nor does the Platonic idea consist in realization of itself: the idea of the good or the equal does not know what goodness or equality is. Neither does the Aristotelian form consist in knowing itself, nor the God of Aristotle, despite its definition, as I hope we may see, nor the *Logos* of Philo, and Plotinus and St. John the Evangelist, nor the soul of St. Thomas Aquinas. This is, in fact, a notion which is most peculiar to modernity.

If I may be taken *cum grano salis* I will say that the manner of being of all these things, far from consisting of being for its own sake, or knowing its own self, consists rather of the opposite, in being for another. Red is

red for someone who sees it, and Platonic goodness, perfect goodness, *is* that for anyone who may be capable of
thinking it. Therefore the ancient world ended among the
neo-Platonists of Alexandria, by a searching for Plato's
ideal objects on the part of anyone for whom they existed or had to exist, and that one put them forth tenta-
tively and confusedly as contents of the divine mind. As
a whole, the ancient world knew only one manner of
being, which consisted in exteriorizing itself, hence in
opening itself up, in displaying itself, in directing itself
toward the outside. It follows that the revelation of being
(this the truth) they would call "discovery," ἀλήδεια,
manifestation, denuding. But Cartesian thought, on the
contrary, consists of being for the sake of being, of taking an account of oneself, therefore of being directed toward one's own interior, of reflecting on oneself, of
putting oneself within oneself. Compared with the self
which is directed outwards, the ostentatious exterior self
that the ancients knew, there arose this manner of being
which consisted essentially of being within oneself, of
being pure intimacy and reflectiveness. For so strange
a reality it was necessary to find a new name; the word
"soul" would not serve, for the ancient soul was no less
external than was the body, as in Aristotle; and in St.
Thomas Aquinas it was still a principle of bodily vitality.
Hence the great problem for St. Thomas was the definition of angels—that they are souls without a body when
the Aristotelian definition of the soul includes bodily
vitality.

But the *cogitatio* has nothing to do with the body. For
the moment, my body is only an idea held within my
mind. The soul is neither in nor with the body, but the
idea of body is within my mind, within my soul. If, in
addition, it turns out that the body is a reality outside of

me, a sizable reality, effectively material and not ideal—
this means that body and soul, matter and mind, have
nothing to do with one another, cannot touch each other
or enter into any direct relation with each other. In
Descartes for the first time the material and the spiritual
world are separated by their very essence—the being as
the essence of the external and the being as something
essentially internal are henceforth defined as incompatible. There could be no greater contrast and conflict with
ancient philosophy. For Plato, as for Aristotle, matter
and what they called spirit (for us, grandchildren of
Descartes as we are, it was pseudo-spirit) were defined
as one defines right and left, inverse and reverse—matter
was what receives spirit, and spirit was what gives form
to matter—thus the one was defined in relation to the
other, and not as does the modern, who defines the one
in contradiction to the other, by excluding the other.

The name which, after Descartes, is given to thought
as being for itself, as realizing, recognizing itself, is conscience or the conscious. Not soul, spirit, *psyche*, which
means air or a breath—because it animates the body,
breathes life into it, moves it as a sea breeze pushes the
sail in curving it—but conscience, that is, taking account
of oneself. In this term there appears openly the constituent attribute of thought, which is knowing oneself,
holding to oneself, reflecting on oneself, entering into
oneself, being *withinness*.

Conscience, the conscious, is reflection, withinness,
and nothing else. When we say "I" we express the same
thing. On saying "I," I speak to myself: I place my being
only in reference to myself, that is, by referring myself
only to me. I am I in the measure in which I return to
myself, in which I withdraw into my own being—not
going forth outside it, but on the contrary in a perpetual

movement of return. Therefore, when we say "I," we turn the index finger toward our breasts, not deliberately, but symbolizing in this visible pantomime our invisible returning and reflective essence. Hence the Stoics, whose formation of ideas was always materialistic, saw in the gesture proof that man's illustrious soul, his "I," lived in his outward self. The "I" is the gerfalcon that returns always to its master—its master being itself—and its whole existence is this swooping gesture of flight toward its own depths. The bird which, leaving space and the firmament, annuls space with its flight, coming back to itself, folding itself within itself—the wing at once a wing and its own air—we might call it a flight that is a nonflight, an undoing of natural flight. To discover so strange a reality as the conscious—does this not imply turning one's back on life, is it not taking an attitude which is completely opposed to that which is natural to us in living? Is it not natural to live outwardly, directed toward the world about us, to believe in its reality, to lean on the magnificent circumference of the horizon as on an immovable arch which upholds us as though floating above existence? How does man reach this discovery, how does he achieve that anti-natural twist, turn toward himself and on turning find his intimate self, recognize that it is only that, only reflection, intimacy?

But there is something more serious: if the conscious is one's intimate self, if it is seeing oneself and holding to oneself, it will be an exclusive commerce with oneself. Consequently Descartes, although without ultimate clarity, cuts the cables which unite us and mix us with the world—with bodies, with other men; he makes of each mind a private precinct. But he does not emphasize what this means: to be a private enclosure does not mean only that nothing external can penetrate into the soul, that the world does not send us its enriching reality, but it also means the reverse: that the mind treats only with itself, that it cannot go forth from itself—that the conscious is not only a private preserve but that it is also the retreat of a recluse. Therefore that on finding our own true selves we find that we are alone in the Universe, that each "I" is in its very essence solitude, fundamental solitude.

With this we have set a foot on *terra incognita*. On beginning this course I said that I was moved to communicate the maturity of certain thoughts, many of them new. I repeat my promise to discuss a basic innovation in philosophy. Tomorrow we will start to move into this *terra incognita*.

8

The Discovery of Subjectivity. Ancient "Ecstasy" and "Spiritualism." The Two Roots of Modern Subjectivity. The Transcendent God of Christianity.

THE decisive discovery of the conscious, of subjectivity, of the "I," was not finally achieved until Descartes appeared. As we saw, this discovery consisted in finding that among the things existing or pretending to exist in the Universe there is one whose manner of being differentiates it radically from the others: this is thought. What do we mean when we say of this theatre that it exists? What, in one interpretation or another, do we finally understand by the existence of things? This theatre exists, that is to say, there it is. But what does "there" mean? "There" means there in the world, there in the Universe, in the general ambit of realities. This theatre exists; that is to say, it is a bit of Madrid, supported on the great piece of earth which is Castile, which in turn is supported on the other greater thing called planet, which is supported in the astronomic system, and so on. Insofar as "being there" is concerned, the existence of things is a matter of some of them resting on others, therefore of some of them being *on* the others, some of them being placed on top of others. In this sense the existence of things has a somewhat static meaning and becomes almost a matter of lying on top of one another. Is it not this which we really understand by "being there"?

On the other hand, when I say that a thought of mine exists, I do not understand by its existence a "being there" but quite the contrary: my thought exists *when* and *because* I recognize it, that is to say, when I think it; it exists in itself and for itself. But if my thought exists only *when* and *because* I think it, that is, when I execute it, when I make it, the result will be that its existence is not like that of a thing, a mere matter of lying on top of, a passively being on something else, a simple process of forming part of a collection of things lying each on top of another, a group of quietudes, but thought will be existence as an active process of being—therefore thought is not a matter of location, not a being here or being there, but a constant making and remaking of itself, an incessant actuating. This means that the discovery of what is most peculiar about thinking brings with it the discovery of a manner of being which is fundamentally different from that of things. If by "thing" we understand something which in the last analysis is more or less static, the manner of being that is inherent in thought consists in pure bringing into action, pure agility, in self-generated movement. Thought is the true, the unique and only automotive force, self-powered and self-propelled.

Thought consists, we said, in reflection, in reflecting on itself, in taking account of itself. But this assumes that there is in thought a duality, that it doubles on itself; that there is reflected thought and thought reflecting. It is well for us to analyze, however quickly, the minimal elements which integrate all thinking so that we may gain clarity about certain concepts which are very much used in modern philosophy, such as subject, the "I," or self, the contents of the conscious, and so on. It is well for us to have them ready, clean, disinfected, so to speak, because thought certainly recognizes things other than itself. Thus we are now seeing this theatre, and while we do no more than live during the process of this seeing, it seems to us that the theatre exists outside and apart from us. But now we note that this was a problematical belief ascribed to every act of unconscious thought, that is to say, to every act of thinking which ignores itself. To the victim of hallucination, the theatre as hallucination does not seem to exist with any lesser degree of reality than does the one we now have before us. This makes us recognize that seeing is not a process in which the subject goes outside himself and puts himself magically into contact with reality itself. For the moment, the theatre of hallucination and the authentic theatre both exist within me, and nowhere else; they are states of my mind, they are *cogitationes* or thoughts. They are—as men began to say about the end of the eighteenth century and have been saying up to our own day—contents of the conscious, of the self, of the thinking subject. Every other reality of things beyond that which we hold as our own ideas is problematical, and, at best, derived from this primary reality which we possess as contents of the conscious. The outside world is within us, it exists in our power of formulating ideas. The world is my production, and my image—as the rough Schopenhauer will say roughly. The ideal is the real. Strictly speaking, and in pure truth, only the idea-producing, the thinking, the conscious exists; I, I myself, *me ipsum*.

In me, of course, appear the most varied landscapes; all that I believed myself ingenuously to have about me, all in the midst of which I thought I was, and on which I leaned, is now reborn as fauna and flora within me. They are states of my subjectivity. To see is not to go forth outside oneself, but to find within oneself the image of this theatre, a bit of the image called Universe. The conscious is always with one, it is at once the house and the tenant, it is within-ness—the basic and superlative withinness of myself with myself. This inner-ness of which I consist and which I am makes of me a being closed against the outside, having no windows, no peepholes. If there were windows or peepholes in me the air would enter from the outside, the supposed exterior reality would invade me, and then there would surely be within me things which are alien to me—there would be people in me—and I would not be pure and exclusive within-ness. But this discovery of my being as that which is within, affording me the delight of being in contact with my own self rather than of seeing myself merely as one exterior thing among all the other things, has on the other hand the inconvenience that it shuts me up within myself, makes of me at once a prison and a prisoner. I am perpetually arrested within myself. I am Universe, but at the same time I am one—alone. The element of which I am made, the thread of which I am woven, is solitude.

This is where we stopped the other day. The idealist thesis, mistress of culture during the entire modern age, is undoubtedly most firm, but at the same time, if seen from the point of view of the good bourgeois and of daily life, it is frenetic. There could be no greater paradox: it turns upside down the manner of thinking about the Universe which is familiar in a nonphilosophic life. At the same time, it is an excellent example of that intellectual heroism which I presented some time ago as characteristic of the process of philosophizing. It is arrival without pity at the final consequences which our reasoning demands, it is a journey to the far point where pure theory leads us. Including the possibility that it may lead us to a point that the good bourgeois, who always lives on one of the floors of our own person, will call absurd and will refuse to accept.

But there is something extraordinarily strange in this idealist thesis, and that is its point of departure, the discovery of subjectivity as such, of thought in its inmost being. Because the fact is that ancient man was completely ignorant of that way of being subjective, reflective, intimate, and solitary.

And I do not know which is the more curious—the fact that ancient man failed to know his own being, his subjective self, or the fact that modern man discovers the self as he would discover a most unexpected continent. The theme is important and new, but it is difficult of treatment. I do not know whether I am going to be able to clarify it for you. The only thing I know is that I am going to try it most loyally.

If, starting from our present mode of thinking which has already discovered the conscious and the subjective, self-centered being, we draw our interior selves in the shape of a circle, whatever there is in us and what happens to us will fill this circle. The center of this circle will be symbolized by that element of our consciousness which we call the "I"; its role lies in being the subject of all our acts, of seeing and hearing, of imagining, thinking, loving and hating. All those mental acts have this in common, that they seem to emanate or radiate from a central point which is present and active in all of them. In all seeing, someone sees; in all loving, someone loves; in all thinking, someone thinks. This someone we call "I," the self. And this "I" which sees or thinks is not a reality apart from the seeing and the thinking, but merely the ingredient called *subject* which forms part of every act.

If the "I" can be symbolized as the center of our consciousness, our awareness, the periphery of the circle will be occupied by everything else in us, that is, by all the images of sounds, colors, forms, bodies, by all that external world which presents itself as surrounding us, and which we call nature or cosmos.

In the life of man this cosmic periphery made up of material things is constantly asking for attention. Attention is a basic activity of the "I" which directs and regulates all the rest of its activities. Thus in order to exercise the act of seeing and hearing something it is not enough to have it in front of us. Those who live near a cataract eventually cease to hear it, and this very moment we are seeing only a part of what constitutes the visible section of this theatre, the part on which we fix our attention, the portion to which we attend. All seeing is a looking, a seeking with the eyes; all hearing is a listening, an attending with the ears.

So I say that nature, the external world, solicits man's attention with a terrible urgency, constantly setting before him the problems of subsistence and defense. Human existence, especially in the primitive ages of mankind, is an unending war with nature, with things, and the individual cannot rest from it by turning to any other form of work than that which will solve the needs of his material life. This means that man attends only to the periphery of his being, to the visible and the tangible. He lives without giving heed to more than his cosmic surroundings. The "I" is out there where his attention is fixed; the rest does not exist for it. In our symbolic representation we would say that the only part of the circle which exists is the line that defines it—that is, that the subjective goes no deeper than the circumference. Once in a while a bodily pain, an inner anguish draws attention back from the periphery toward the interior of the circle, from nature toward the self, but only for a fugitive moment. Attention, not trained to direct itself within, tends always toward its first and habitual direction and goes back to grasping at surrounding things. This is what we may call the "natural" attitude of consciousness, for which *only* the cosmic world, composed of corporeal things, exists. Man lives alert on his own frontiers, looking toward the outside, absorbed in nature, attentive to the external.

In the always problematical measure in which we can imagine to ourselves the souls of animals, we would say that their internal situation would somewhat resemble that of "natural" man. Remember that the animal is always alert. The ears of a horse in the field, like two live antennae, two periscopes, reveal in their restlessness the fact that the animal is always preoccupied with what lies about him. Look at the monkeys in their cage at the zoo. It is marvelous how these man-apes are into everything. Nothing that happens around them escapes them. The word "ecstasy" means, etymologically, to be outside oneself. In this sense the animal lives in a perpetual state of ecstasy, kept outside himself by the urgency of external dangers. To turn inward toward himself would be to have his attention distracted from what is happening on the outside, and such distraction might carry with it the risk of the animal's death. Nature in its pristine glory is fierce: it tolerates no distractions. One must be possessed of a hundred eyes, constantly ready to challenge with a "Who goes there?"; quick to receive news of surrounding changes, so as to respond with movements that are adequate to the demand. Attention to nature is life in action. The pure animal is the pure man of action.

Thus primitive man lives in advance of himself, his attention nailed to the cosmic scene, leaving his own self at his back. The "I" concerns itself directly with things; as the sun's ray pierces the crystal, neither halting within it nor heeding it, so the "I" pierces its own inner volume, going straight to things and occupying itself with them. This is how, and why, the primary and natural thing, from a biological point of view, is that man should ignore himself.

The surprising thing, the fact which intrigues one and demands clarification, is the opposite one. How is it that man's attention, which is primarily centrifugal and directed toward the periphery, could execute that unlikely twist on itself by which the "I," turning its back on the surrounding world, sets itself to look inside itself? It will soon occur to you that this phenomenon of introversion presupposes two things—one which incites the subject to free himself from the outside and the other which calls his attention to his own internal self. The one without the other will not suffice. If attention is merely freed from its service to the outside it may seek refuge in other things. But the simple act of turning away from the external does not carry with it the discovery of and preference for the internal. In order that a woman may fall in love with one man it is not enough that she falls out of love with another; the former must somehow manage to attract her attention.

But before entering on a brief clarification of an event so decisive for humanity, we might find it useful to recall the description which we have given of the native and primary attitude of the mind in order to understand the mode of thinking which was dominant in Greek—and in general in all ancient—philosophy. The major advance which has been achieved in these last years in history, and especially in the history of philosophy, consists in having allowed ourselves the luxury of sincerity in recognizing that we do not understand the ancient thinkers. This sincerity with ourselves, as is always the case with such sincerity, has been repaid *ipso facto*. Once recognizing that we were not understanding them, we then began for the first time actually to understand them, that is to say, to note that they were thinking in a form which is different from ours, and then in consequence to seek the key formula in that mode of thinking. This is not a matter of whether their doctrines were different from ours in greater or lesser degree, but of the fact that their mental attitude was different.

In essence, ancient man kept the texture of primitive man. Like him, ancient man lived concerned with things, and the only cosmos existing for him was the cosmos of bodies. He might by chance achieve glimpses of what lies within him, but as glimpses they were unstable and in effect fortuitous. In attitude, the Greek mind is rigorously primitive—except that the Greek was not content with focusing his entire attention on the external world; he philosophized about it, elaborated concepts which transcribed into pure theory all the reality around him. Greek ideas were molded into a reality of external and corporeal things. The very word "idea" and its relatives means "visible figure," "aspect." As in addition to bodies there are in nature the movements and changes of bodies, the Greek had to think of other invisible and immaterial things out of which movement and corporeal change proceed. These immaterial things were finally thought of as material things, rarefied and refined, taking the form of spirits.

Thus the animal consists of matter which is organized

and moved about by a thing which is within it, hidden in the matter; this is the soul. But this soul has nothing of the inner self, it is internal only in the sense that it is hidden within the body, submerged in it, and therefore invisible. It is a breath, a light breeze, ψυχή—or, as in Thales, a bit of humidity, or as in Heraclitus, fire. Although the modern has kept the word "spirit" to designate his discovery of the inner self, it is well to note that the Greek and the Latin understood by this term a reality which was no less external than bodies and ascribed to bodies, a power lodged in the cosmic. Certainly in Aristotle the human soul has powers not possessed by the animal soul, just as the animal soul has qualities which the vegetable soul lacks, but, as for souls in the Greek way of thinking, the human is no more of a soul than is the vegetable. Thus the human soul is at the same time and *pro indiviso* a power both of reasoning and of vegetating. So it is not strange that Aristotle places the science of the soul, psychology, as part of biology.

Aristotle's psychology groups man and the plant together because the soul for him is not a principle of the innermost being, but a cosmic principle of bodily vitality, even more, or even less, a principle of movement and change, since for the Greek there exists even a mineral soul—the soul of every celestial body. The Greek idea of the soul most nearly resembles an occult power, but external in itself, which we suppose ingenuously to be a matter of magnetism in order to explain the attractions which its visible body exercises. That one should still talk seriously today of Aristotle's "spiritualism" in the modern sense of the word "spirituality" would be merely a bit of historical innocence if it were not so insincere. Because if by forcing the texts one introduces into the Aristotelian spirit our modern concept of the conscious, then this insincerity is inverted and includes a failure to confess that it is meaningless; for according to Aristotle the stars have a soul, that is, a conscious, and as a conscious consisting only in pure recognition of itself, it can move the heavy bulk of a sidereal body.

The Greek did not discover the soul as an inner vision of himself, but he found it on the outside as an almost corporeal entity. Hence he interprets sense perception, and with it the whole of intellectual life, as an impact between bodies; corporeal things collide with the thing called soul and leave on it the impress of their figures. Before these collisions with things, the soul held nothing, it was a tablet of wax that was still intact. So far from withinness, from self-justification, is this Greek soul which can exist empty, undented, like a photographic plate focused toward the outside, on which nothing is printed that does not come to it from the outside, poured forth and deposited on it by nature! What a distance there is between this soul and the baroque monad of Leibnitz, into which nothing can enter and from which nothing can come forth, but which lives on itself, an original spring feeding on its own inner richness! Another day I would very much like to talk more in detail about this ancient manner of thinking. But now we must hurry back to our subject.

How is it that man's attention, which is naturally centrifugal, twists and turns back on itself a hundred and eighty degrees and instead of moving toward the outside fixes its attention on the subject itself? What happened that human eyes should have turned inward toward man, as the eyes of damaged dolls turn toward the inside of their own papier mâché heads?

Without sound or bloodshed, lacking cymbals to announce it, fifes to exalt it, or poets to adorn it with verses, this shift is undoubtedly one of the greatest events for which the planet has provided a stage. Ancient man still lived close to his brother the animal, and like him, was focused toward the external. Modern man has put himself inside himself, has turned within himself, has awakened from his cosmic unconsciousness, shaken off the sleep which was left to him from the garden, the algae, the mammal, and has taken possession of himself; he has discovered himself. Some fine day he will step out as usual, and find that he has tripped against a strange, unknown, and unaccustomed thing; he will not see it clearly, but he will push against it, and will note that it is he who feels the hurt, he who is at once the pusher and the pushed—that he has collided with himself. "It hurts me, therefore I exist." *Cogito, sum*. A devilish adventure! Devilish? Is it not rather divine? Is it not most probable that in so extraordinary an event God has taken the trouble to intervene very specially? But which God? The Christian God? Yes, the Christian, only the Christian God. But how would the Christian God have personally intervened in the specifically modern discovery from which the whole anti-Christian age springs as from a seed? This possibility disturbs the Christians and irritates the anti-Christians, the moderns.

The Christian is anti-modern: he has set himself comfortably, once and for all, against modernity. He does not accept it. It is the child of Satan. And now he is told that modernity is a ripe fruit of the idea of God. The modern, for his part, is anti-Christian: he believes that modernity was born in opposition to the religious idea. Now, for the very reason that he is modern, he is invited to recognise himself as a son of God. This irritates him. It is turning history upside down, it is proposing a change of convictions. The anti-Christian and the anti-modern do not want to be forced to change; they prefer inertia. We have seen that being is pure agility, incessant movement. The anti-Christian and the anti-modern do not wish to move, do not wish to be; hence they are content with a state of anti-being.

The discovery of subjectivity has two deep historic roots, one negative and the other positive. The negative root is skepticism, the positive is Christianity. Neither the one without the other, nor the other without the one, could have produced such a result.

As we have had occasion to note, doubt or *skepsis*, σχέψις, is the condition of scientific knowledge; it opens the crack which proof will fill. The Greeks, who were masters of theorizing, exercised that virtue of doubting in a fashion which was exemplary and they played it to the end. Above all, the schools called skeptic left in this field nothing for later times to do. No one could doubt of more than the academicians doubted—neither Descartes, nor Hume, nor Kant developed a more superior skepticism. On both the active and the passive side they demonstrated the illusory character of knowledge. We cannot know what things are. At most we are able to say what they seem to us to be. But it is clear that the Greek skeptics are . . . Greeks, and as knowledge is the knowledge of being, and being for the Greek takes no other form than that which is external, the whole of Greek skepticism has reference to our knowledge of cosmic reality.

They reach formulae which are quite literally modern, which say marvelously what no modern would say better. Thus the Cyrenaics will say that we cannot know the real because the soul cannot go forth outside itself but is enclosed within its own territories—εἰς τὰ πάδη χατέχλεισαν ἑαυτούς—and lives as within a beleaguered city—ὥσπερ ἐν πολιορχία. Is not this the discovery of the innermost? Could there be a more precise, and at the same time more plastic expression of the subjective being? A mistake! The Greek who thought that does not see the positive element in it. With those words he means that we cannot depart from the real—but it does not occur to him that in this inability to go forth, this being shut within ourselves, there is a new reality, firmer and more fundamental than external reality. There are few examples in history which show more clearly that for the discovery of a new thing, intellectual keenness is not enough. One must have enthusiasm for this, a previous love for this very thing. Understanding is a lantern which must go directed by a hand, and the hand must be moved by a pre-existent eagerness for this or that type of possible things. In short, one finds only what one seeks, and what understanding finds is thanks to what love seeks. Hence, all the sciences began by being the particular enthusiasms of their enthusiasts.

Contemporary pedantry has deprived this word enthusiast—*aficionado*—of its prestige; but enthusiast is the utmost than one can be with respect to a thing, it is the source, the germ of everything. And we would say the same thing of the word *dilettante*, which means a lover. Love seeks so that understanding may find. This is a great theme for a long and fertile conversation which would consist in demonstrating how the being that seeks is the very essence of love! Did you ever think about the surprising texture of seeking? He who seeks does not have, he does not even know what he seeks, and on the other hand, to seek is to assume the thing sought and indeed to have it by prevision. To seek is to anticipate a reality which is still nonexistent.

He who fixes his attention only on what awakes and fires love does not understand what love is. If the love of a woman is born of her beauty, it is not pleasure in that beauty which constitutes love and the process of loving. Once awakened, love consists in the constant beaming forth of a favorable atmosphere, a loyal and affectionate light in which we envelop the beloved being, so that all her other qualities and perfections can reveal themselves, make themselves manifest, and we will recognize them. Hatred, on the contrary, puts the hated being in a negative light, and we see only its defects. Love, then, prearranges and prepares the possible perfections of the beloved. Hence it enriches us by making us see what we would not see without it. Above all, the love of a man for a woman is like an attempt at transmigration, at going beyond ourselves, it inspires migratory tendencies within us.

But let us leave these impassioned journeys and anchor ourselves anew in our subject. We have seen how skepticism teaches man not to believe in the reality of the outside world, and consequently to lose interest in it. But in this first act he remains, blind, on the doorstep of internal man. As Herbart said, "Every good beginner is a skeptic, but every skeptic is only a beginner."

The positive motive is lacking, and the interest in subjectivity by which this latter would draw attention back to itself and install itself in the limelight. This lack is Christianity's doing. The Greek gods are no more than supreme cosmic authorities, towering summits of external reality, sublime natural powers. In a pyramid the apex dominates the whole structure, but at the same time it is a part of that pyramid. Thus the gods of the Greek religion are above the world, but they form part of it and they are its finest flower. The god of the river and the forest, the god of grain and of the lightning are the divine froth of these intramundane realities.

The Hebrew God walks with the thunder and the lightning. But the Christian God has nothing to do with either the lightning or the river, the grain or the thunder. He is a God of transcendent and extramundane truth, whose manner of being is not to be compared with that of any cosmic reality. Nothing about Him, not even the tips of His toes, is part of this world, or even tangent to this world. For this reason the Christian's highest mystery is the incarnation. That a God utterly incommensurable with the world should put himself into that world "and abide among us" is the greatest paradox. This which is, speaking logically, a mystery for Christianity was for Greek mythology a matter of daily history. At every hour of the day the gods of Olympus took earthly, and at times infrahuman form, they became the swan trembling over Leda, or the bull which ran with Europa on his back.

But the Christian God is transcendent. He is *deus exsuperantissimus*. Christianity proposes to man that he enter into contact with such a being. How is such contact possible? Not only is it impossible by means of or through the world and intra-worldly things, but everything in the world becomes for the moment a handicap and a barrier to any contact with God. In order to stand with God one must begin by doing away with virtually everything which is cosmic and earthly, accepting it as nonexistent, for in the face of God it is actually nothing. And this is where the soul, in order to approach God, in its eagerness for contact with divinity, in order to save itself, will act as does the skeptic with his methodic doubt. It denies the reality of the world, of other beings, of the state, of society, of man's own body. And only when he has suppressed all this does man begin to feel himself truly a live being. Why? For the very reason that the soul has remained alone, alone with God. Christianity is the discoverer of solitude as the substance of the soul. I say this formally: as the substance of the soul. No one of you now listening to me knows what that means. Solitude as substance! What is that? Patience, please. I hope that at this stage I may be spared guesses, but not the bright light of clarity. Have no doubt that at the proper moment this expression will be made clear.

The soul is truly itself when it remains without a world, freed from it, therefore when it is alone. And there is no other form of entering into company with God except through solitude, because only under the shadow of solitude does the soul meet with its own authentic being. God, and facing Him, the solitary soul—there is no other true reality from the Christian point of view, in the Christian religion (not the so-called "Christian philosophy" which is, as we shall see, a sad and useless chain which Christianity drags behind it). There is only that double reality, God and the soul—and as knowledge for the Christian is always knowledge of the real, the finest knowledge will be of God and the soul. Thus, St. Augustine: *"Deum et animam scire cupio. Nihilne plus? Nihil omnino"* (I desire to know about God and the soul. Nothing more? Nothing less).

It is not chance that St. Augustine should be the first thinker who glimpsed the fact of consciousness and the self as the secret innermost; neither is it chance that he should be the first to stumble on that truth that one cannot doubt that he doubts. It is curious that the founder of Christian ideology and the founder of modern philosophy should so coincide in their whole first line. For St. Augustine, too, the self exists insofar as it knows itself to be—its being is its knowing—and that reality of thought is first in the order of theoretic truths. One must take one's stand on that reality, not on the problematical reality of the cosmos and that which is external. *"Noli foras ire, in te ipsum redi: in interiori homine habitat veritas"* (Do not go afar; seek within thyself. Truth resides inside of man). Here, too, is man as absolute interior, as the innermost. And like Descartes, in the depth of this innermost being he finds God. It is curious that all religious men should coincide in talking to us of what St. Theresa too calls "the depths of the soul"; and that it should be just in that depth of the soul where, without going forth from it, they find God. The Christian God is apparently transcendent to the world, but immanent in the "depths of the soul." Is there any reality behind this somewhat dusty metaphor? Let us not ask questions now which we cannot now answer.

Nevertheless it would be false and unjust to affirm that Descartes is already apparent in St. Augustine. However many more coincidences can be proved between them, the distance between them will still be enormous. St. Augustine was a genius of religious sensibility; through his religious intuition he comes to discover the reflective being—as a philosopher he manages to define his intuition and to put it in the place which corresponds to it in science, but as he is not the great philosopher that Descartes is, he lacks the sudden stroke of genius which leads the latter to turn the whole of ancient ideology upside down and to found modern idealism. But there is one most important difference: St. Augustine, who is already a modern—with Julius Caesar, the only modern of the old Mediterranean world—is also an ancient. And along with his new ideas, neither separate nor distinct from them, comes the whole ancient mental attitude. Hence his philosophy is chaotic, hence he is a father of the Church, but not a classic of philosophy.

It has not yet been demonstrated, on the other hand, that Descartes, apparently a man of very little reading, was acquainted with the work of St. Augustine or took suggestions from him. But this does not matter. The hint was in the air. The idea of the conscious which flowered in St. Augustine goes on maturing throughout the entire Middle Ages, within the limits of that scholasticism which had such contempt for it because the scholastics never even studied it, not even in the form that was due to the surviving scholastics. The chain of transmission from St. Augustine to Descartes can be reconstructed— passing through St. Bernard of Clairvaux, through the Victorines, St. Bonaventura and the Franciscans, Duns Scotus, Occam, and Nicholas of Autrecourt. Along this road the idea of the conscious loomed only once; with St. Thomas Aquinas, who abandoned this idea, originally Christian, in order to return to Aristotle's cosmic soul, thus forcing Christianity's original inspiration back into the incongruous mold of ancient thinking. Modernity was born out of Christianity; let there be no battle between the ages, let them all be sisters, and welcome! Here is where my lecture should begin today, but the exploring of that *terra incognita* which we had reached earlier remains for another day.

9

The Theme of Our Times. A Fundamental Reform of Philosophy. The Basic Fact of the Universe. Myself for the World, and the World for Me. The Life of Every One of Us.

WE have before us today a serious task, serious within the always sportive and jovial atmosphere with which all philosophy should surround itself if it aims to be philosophic rather than pedantic. Today we must more than ever sharpen our concepts, have them shining, clean, and disinfected, because they are going to serve us as instruments in a surgical operation.

We have been tracing the purest version of the magnificent idealist thesis which inspired modernity, that body of thought in which all of us, directly or by opposition, have been educated, and which still constitutes the prevailing order in human culture. When idealism left the reality of the outside world hanging in suspense and discovered the primordial reality of the conscious, of subjectivity, it lifted philosophy to a new level from which the latter cannot slip back under pain of retrogression in the worst sense of the word. Ancient realism, which starts from the undoubted existence of cosmic things, is philosophic ingenuousness, the innocence of Paradise. All innocence is paradisiac. Because the innocent, he who neither doubts, distrusts, nor suspects, finds himself in the position of ancient and primitive man, surrounded by nature, a cosmic landscape, a garden—and this is Paradise.

Doubt throws man out of Paradise, out of external reality. And where does this absolute Adam, which is thought, go when he sees himself thrown out of the Cosmos? He has nowhere to put himself, he must come to grips with himself, must thrust himself within himself. Out of Paradise, which signifies the kind of attention to the external that is proper to the child, he moves to *ensimismamiento*, within-ness, attention to that which is innermost, the melancholy of youth. The Modern Age is melancholic, and the whole of it is more or less romantic. St. Augustine, who was the first romantic, formidable and gigantic in everything he touched, is the soul of philosophic candor.* Whatever may be our own inten-

---

*St. Augustine was the first romantic, gigantic and formidable in every respect, including his romanticism, in his capacity for worrying about himself, for tormenting himself, for piercing his own breast with the curved beak of the imperial Roman and Catholic eagle. Adam in Paradise followed by a moaning Adam self-absorbed! And it is curious to recall that as a matter of fact, according to Genesis, when Adam and Eve were exiled from the Garden of Eden the first thing that each discovered was his own person. They became aware of themselves, they discovered the existence of their own beings and they felt a sense of shame because they found themselves naked! And because they thus discovered themselves, they covered themselves with skins. Note this—here the fact of covering themselves is the direct consequence of discovering themselves. Apparently when man encounters his conscious self, his own subjectivity, he realizes that this cannot exist in the open air, in contact with the outside, like the rock, the plant, or the beast, but that the human self is what it is for the very reason that it separates itself from its surroundings, is closed within itself. The "I" is a covered and intimate self, and

tions, our designs for innovation and philosophic progress, it must be understood that we cannot slip back from idealism to the ingenuous realism of the Greeks or the scholastics. It is pertinent to remember the egregious motto of Cromwell's soldiers: *"Vestigia nulla retrorsum."*

We go beyond idealism, therefore we leave it behind us like a stretch of road which we have already passed, like a city in which we have once lived and which we keep forever lodged in our souls. We carry idealism with us, that is to say, we hold onto it, we preserve it. Idealism was a step upwards in the intellectual ascent; now we put a foot up on another step which is not below idealism but above it.

But in order to do this we must submit idealism to a surgical operation. In the idealist thesis the "I," the self, the subject, swallows the outside world. In this process of ingurgitation the self has swollen. The idealist self has become a tumor; we must operate on it.

We will employ most exquisite care and all the necessary asepsis. But this intervention was necessary. The self was ill, very ill—for the very reason that everything was going well for it. For the Greek, the self was a mere detail in the Cosmos. Hence Plato almost never uses the word "ego." At most he will say ἡμεῖς, "we"—that is, the social community, the Athenians as a public body, or the lesser group of his followers at his Academy. For Aristotle, the "I-soul" is like a hand—ὡς χείρ—which

the garment is the symbol of the frontier that separates the "I" from all the rest of the world. But I said that covering oneself is the immediate consequence of discovering oneself. I put it badly. Another thing is interposed between the one and the other. Adam, on discovering himself, is ashamed of himself, and because he is ashamed he covers himself. The thing that is immediate, that is one and the same thing with discovering oneself, is being ashamed of oneself. What does this mean? Is shame in all seriousness the form in which the "I" discovers itself? Is this the authentic consciousness of oneself?

touches the Cosmos, shapes itself to the Cosmos in order
to inform itself about the Cosmos, as the imploring hand
of a blind man slips between things in order to examine
them. But in Descartes, the self is already rising to the
rank of a primary theoretic truth, and when Leibnitz
makes of it a *monad*, closed within itself and set aside
from the great Cosmos, it becomes an intimate little
world, a microcosmos, and is, according to Leibnitz himself, a "*petit Dieu*," a *microteos*. And as idealism reaches
its culmination in Fichte, so in him the self touches the
zenith of its destiny and becomes the entire Universe,
everything.

The self has enjoyed a brilliant career. It cannot complain. It could not be more than it is. Yet nevertheless it
does complain, and with reason. Because when it took
the world within itself the modern self was left alone.
You remember that the Emperor of China, by virtue
of his own superior rank, could have no equals, and
hence no friends who would have had to have been his
equals—therefore one of his titles was "the solitary man."
Idealism's self is Europe's Emperor of China. Insofar as
is possible the self would like to overcome its solitude
even at the cost of not being all-powerful; what it wants
now is to be a little less in order to live a little more—
to have things about it which are different, other and
different selves with whom to converse, that is to say,
"you" and "he" and above all, that "you" which is most
completely different from "I," that "you" which is "she,"
or for the feminine "I," the "you" which turns out to
be "he."

In short, the self needs to go out of itself, to find a
world around it. Idealism has reached the point where
it smothers the sources of vital energies and weakens the
springs of living. It has almost succeeded in convincing

man seriously, which means vitally, that everything around him is only himself and his image. As the primary mind, on the other hand, spontaneous and incorrigible, goes on presenting us with all that effective reality which is very different from us, so idealism has been a rough and tenacious march against the grain of life, an insistent pedagogue trying to make it quite clear to us that to live spontaneously was to suffer an error, an optical illusion.

Even the miser could not enjoy the pleasure of continuing to be a miser if he thought that the piece of gold was only the image of a piece of gold, that is, a counterfeit coin; nor could the gallant continue to be in love with a woman if he were convinced that she was in truth not the woman he thought her, but only her image, a *fantôme d'amour*. Anything else would not be love, but self-love, auto-eroticism. Once we are convinced that the beloved woman is not what we think her to be, but only an image that we ourselves generously made, the catastrophe of disillusion overcomes us. That these are not exaggerations, that even those details of living (and living is composed only of details)—have corrosively penetrated idealism and devitalized life, is a thing which, given more time, I would try to prove to you.

But now we have before us the difficult task of cutting idealism apart, freeing the self from its exclusive prison, providing it with a world around it, curing its absorption in self and insofar as is possible attempting to provide for its escape. *"E quindi uscimmo a riverder le stelle."* But how can the "I" come back out of itself? Will it then not fall back into the ingenuous attitudes of the ancient world? To this I would answer, first, that the coming out would not be a coming out *again;* the ingenuous self of the ancient world had never come out of itself for the simple reason that its ingenuousness lay in the fact that it had never gone into itself. In order to come out, it must have been within. Nor is this merely a play on words. The "I" is, as we saw, one's innermost being; we are now considering the matter of its emerging from itself while still keeping this sense of the innermost. Is this not contradictory? But we are now in the season of reaping and harvest, so that contradiction does not startle us, for we know that every problem rising before us is a dilemma which has two horns. Rather than trying to file off the aggressive second horn, and pretending that no such dilemma exists, let us formulate it in all its fierceness! The "I" is the innermost being, it is that which is within us, it exists for itself. Nevertheless it must, without losing this innermost character, find a world which is fundamentally different from itself and go forth, outside itself, to that world. Therefore the "I" must be at once intimate and exotic, withdrawn and free, a prisoner and at liberty. The problem is startling.

Of course, when it is said that we must move beyond idealism, that the self complains of living like a recluse, that idealism, which humanity once found magnificently exciting, can become injurious to life itself, this does not mean that such reproaches are objections raised against the idealist thesis. If this thesis were completely true, if it did not carry within itself certain difficulties of theory, idealism would, despite those complaints, continue untouched and invulnerable. Desires, wishes, the very vital need for another kind of truth, would come crashing against intelligence, rather than creeping toward it quietly. A truth is not a truth because one desires it, but neither is a truth discovered if one does not desire it; because it is wanted, it is sought. So while the disinterested and independent character of our appetite for truth remains

unstained, it is also true that a man or a period comes to
see this or that truth by virtue of a previous interest
which moves them toward it. Without this there would
be no history. The most disparate and unconnected truths
would fall on man's mind like a burst of birdshot, and
he would not know what to do with them.

Of what use would Einstein's truth have been to Galileo? Truth descends only on him who tries for it, who
yearns for it, who carries within himself, pre-formed,
a mental space where the truth may eventually lodge.
A quarter of a century before the theory of relativity
was achieved, men postulated a four-dimensional physics
having no absolute space or time. The empty space where
Einstein installed himself already existed in Poincaré, as
Einstein himself repeatedly makes clear. With a certain
flavor of skepticism, and in order to deprecate truth,
it is frequently said that the father of truth is desire. Like
all bits of skepticism, this is nonsense. If one wants a
specific bit of truth, one wants it if it is in fact true. The
desire for a truth transcends itself, proves beyond itself,
and goes ahead to seek that truth. Man is entirely aware
of when it is that he wants a truth, and when he only
seeks to create illusions for himself, that is, when he wants
a falsehood.

To say, then, that our era both needs and wants to move
beyond modernity and idealism is only to formulate with
humble words and an air of understatement what would
be meant if, with words far nobler and more weighty,
one were to say that the superseding of idealism is the
great intellectual task, the high historic mission of our
era, the "theme of our time." And to him who asks out
of irritation or disdain, "Why must our time change
things, bring about innovations, go further on? Why
that eagerness, that itch for the new, that desire to modify,

to set new fashions?" as has been said so many times in attacks on me—to this I answer that we are going to discover, with evidence as well as with surprise, that in the strictest sense of the phrase, every period has its task, its mission, its demand for innovation. More than that—much more than that—time is not, in the final analysis, what the clocks measure; but time is quite literally a task, a mission, an innovation.

To try to move beyond idealism is by no means a frivolous idea; on the contrary it is to accept the problem of our time, to accept our destiny. So we are going to battle with our problem, to confront the philosophic bull, the piebald minotaur, which our day presents to us.

We are now about to start on the final turn of our spiral, and as is usual on beginning the new circle we repeat the initial definition of philosophy—knowledge of the Universe, or whatever there is. The first thing we must do is to find what reality, among whatever there may be, is really, undoubtedly existent, that is to say, what in the Universe is given to us. In the mind's native attitude, among both primitive and ancient man, and among ourselves when we are not philosophizing, the cosmos, things, nature, the whole of the corporeal, all this seems given and real. This is what one takes first as real, as being. The ancient philosopher seeks the being of things and invents concepts which interpret their mode of being. But idealism stumbles on the fact that things, the outside, the cosmos, all have another reality, a problematical being which is our thinking about those things, about the outside, the cosmos. And thus a new form of reality comes to light, a new manner of being which is truly primordial and sure, the being which is thought.

While the thing's manner of being has a static character which keeps it quietly being what it is and nothing more, the being of movement as a cosmic reality is an immutable thing, is always "movement" (I refer the real enthusiast to the *Parmenides*, to Plato's *Sophist* and to Book Twelve of Aristotle's *Metaphysics*, to those marvelous original texts, not those desiccated summaries which present that prodigious body of ancient philosophy as though it were dried up and stolid). On the other hand, the being of thought consists not simply in being, but in being for its own sake, in taking account of itself, in seeming to itself to be. Do you not note the basic difference between these two ways of being, that of thought, and that of the thing? Do you not see that we must have ideas which are fundamentally new, categories very different from those of the past, in order to understand, in order to conceive theoretically, scientifically, the reality, or whatever it is, that we call thought? As yet we have only an intuition of it, we are seeing what it has of the genuine, but we have trouble finding the good words with which to describe it and express it, words which will adjust themselves, close as the glove to the hand to what that being has which is peculiar to itself.

Not only do we lack adequate concepts, but language is made by the natural mind for the cosmic being, and ancient philosophy did no more than put a bit of polish on those native concepts of language. In that ideological tradition are we formed, and out of habit old words and ideas come forward to offer themselves as interpreters of this new thing, this mode of being which the modern discovered. So we face no less a matter than to invalidate the traditional meaning of the word "being," and as this is the very root of philosophy, any reform of the idea of being means a radical reform in philosophy. Some of us in Europe have been engaged in this struggle for a long time. The fruit of this labor in its prime maturity is what I wanted to offer in this course. I believe that the innovation offered you herewith is no small thing.

You are invited to drop respect for the most venerable, persistent and intrenched concept which exists in our mental tradition: the concept of being. I announce a checkmate to being as Plato knew it, and Aristotle, Leibnitz, Kant, and even Descartes. Anyone who stays stubbornly tied to a traditional meaning of the phrase "to be," which is just what I intend to reform, cannot understand what I am going to say.

Thought exists in the measure and extent in which it is concerned with itself—it consists of taking account of itself, appearing to itself, reflecting on itself. It is not, then, mere quiet being, but reflection. But someone will say: as you said that movement has a quiet being—because it is, in the last analysis, movement and nothing more—so if thought consists in reflection, the latter, reflection, *is*, has a fixed composition which is quiet and unchanging. This is partly true; reflection, in its turn, is none other than a thought of mine, having no more reality than that of being thought, than seeming to me to be "reflection." And thus successively and on all sides we find that being consists solely in terms of reference to itself, in making itself, in moving toward itself; we find only unease. Do not take this expression metaphorically, but in all seriousness; thought is in its essence unease, restlessness; it is not a static being, but an active giving of itself to itself.

In order that a thought may exist, may have a being, it is enough that it be thought; to think it is to make it, to give it being, and it exists only while and because I think it, make it, execute it, activate it. Insofar as thought might have to be quiet it would cease to be thought, for

I would cease to activate it by thinking.

Do not be startled if a thorough understanding of this strange mode of being slips between your mental fingers. No one can suddenly, all in a minute, overcome thousands of years of habit in reasoning. Surely, in listening to me, you have had fugitive moments in which you thought you were seeing everything clear; then at a point, like an eel, intuition escapes you and you fall back into the mental demands of quiet rather than of unquiet being. Do not let this bother you, for the thing will come before us soon in a form which is complete, plastic and attainable.

Let us go back for the moment to what I hope will not offer difficulties and will seem to us evident. Thought, which exists exclusively in taking account of itself, cannot doubt its own existence; if I think A, it is obvious that thinking about A must exist. Hence the first truth concerning what there is can be put this way—thought exists, *cogitatio est*. Thus we complete our earlier circle. All other realities may be illusory, but this—the illusion itself, the seeming this or that to myself, the thinking—this without any possible doubt does exist.

This is the way Descartes begins. But Descartes does not say it as we do: not "thought exists, *cogitatio est*," but he says—who does not remember? "I think, therefore, I am, I exist." "*Cogito, ergo sum.*" How does this proposition differ from ours? The Cartesian theory has two parts: one says, "I think," the other, "therefore I am." To say, "I think," and to say, "*cogitatio est*," thought exists—is one and the same. The difference, then, between Descartes' phrase and our own stems from the fact that he is not content with what to us seems entirely sufficient. Substituting, as in a mathematical equation, an equal for an equal, we put in place of "I think" the phrase

"thought exists," and then the sense of the Cartesian re-
frain comes clearer—"thought exists, it is; therefore I
exist, I am."

We are in the midst of a surgical operation: the scalpel
has cut deep into the *cogito*, into the very viscera of
idealism. Let us proceed with all due care.

For us to say that thought exists, that it is, includes
saying that my "I," my self, exists and has being. Because
there is no thought which does not contain as one of its
elements a subject who thinks, just as it includes an object
which is thought. If, then, thought exists, and in the sense
in which it exists, its subject, the self, will have to exist,
and so will its object. That sense of existing is what is
genuine and new in thought. My thought is what it is
for the sake of my thought: I am and I exist insofar as
and because I think that I am, and such as I think that
I am. This is the new thing which idealism wanted to
bring to the world, and that is the true spiritualism; the
rest is only magic.

But Descartes, who discovered the fact, and who had
sufficient intuition of the thing called "thought," did not
give up the cosmic categories, and faced with what he
sees, he loses his serenity—that is, faced with a being
which consists merely in "seeming," in pure virtuality,
in the dynamism of reflection. Like an ancient, or a
Thomist scholastic, he needs to hold onto something more
solid, to grasp a cosmic being. And behind that being,
he seeks the thought which consists in mere seeming to
itself, referring to itself, giving an account of itself—a
thing-being, a static entity. Though ceases to be a reality
for him; scarcely had he discovered it as a primary reality
when it was converted into a simple manifestation or
quality of another reality which is latent and static.

Translating the aforesaid into the proper Cartesian

phrase we have this: thought undoubtedly exists, but as it exists in a mere seeming to be itself, in a mere appearance, it is not a reality, a being in the traditional sense of the word. Descartes who, like me, doubted everything, did not agree with me in putting in doubt the truth of the ancient categories and in particular, the classic notion of being—which is his ingenuous notion—needs a reasoning, an enthymeme. If it is indubitable that the appearance of thought exists, one must admit under that appearance a latent reality, something which appears in that appearance, which sustains it and which it truly is. That latent reality I call the "I," the self, my real self I do not see, it is not evident to me—therefore I must reach it through a conclusion; in order to affirm the existence of the self I must pass across the bridge of a "hence." "I think, hence I exist." *Je pense, donc je suis.*

But, who is that "I" which exists? *Je ne suis qu'une chose qui pense.* Ah, a thing! The "I" is not thought, but a thing of which thought is an attribute, a manifestation, a phenomenon. We have fallen back into the inert being of Greek ontology. In the same phrase, in the same gesture with which Descartes discovers a new world for us, he withdraws it from us and annuls it. He has the intuition, the vision of being for its own sake, but he conceives it in the Greek manner as a being with substance. This duality, this internal contradiction and painful lack of congruence with itself, has been the essence of idealism and modernity, has been Europe itself.

Up to the present moment Europe has lived bewitched, enchanted by Greece, which is in truth enchanting. But out of all that is Greek let us imitate only Ulysses, and of Ulysses only the grace with which he knew how to escape from the enchantments of Circe and Calypso, prone on their spray-blown islands, with much of the siren about them, and something of Madame Récamier lying full length on her chaise longue. And the skill of Ulysses which Homer does not reveal to us, but which the old Mediterranean sailors knew full well, was that the only dexterous way to free oneself from the fatal song which the sirens sang was to sing one back in return. (In parenthesis, Ulysses is the first Don Juan; fleeing from his everyday Penelope, he finds all the enchanting creatures of our sea, he meets them, he falls in love with them, and he flees from them.)

The sway of Greece has ended; the Greeks are not classic, they are merely archaic—archaic and—certainly this—always marvelous. By the same token, they interest us much more. No longer will they be our pedagogues, they are going to become our friends. We are going to talk with them; we are going to contradict them at the most essential points.

The question which is undoubtedly the most important and difficult in philosophy and which moreover is absolutely new—the question, I say, stems from the following: let us imagine that before discovering our subjective selves we think that for us there can be no reality other than the things we see about us. Let us see what kind of idea we would have about the being of those things. For example, the horse that we see in the Circus—what is the being, the thing that is that horse? We have before us his shape, his color, the resistance offered by his body. Is that the horse's being, its reality? Yes and no. The horse is not its shape alone, because it is also its color, and so on. Color and shape and resistance to touch are things which differ in themselves. The horse is all of them together, or better, a unit, a thing in which those other things are joined. But that thing in which color, form, and so on are united is not yet visible. I assume it, I invent it, it is my interpretation of the observable fact which consists in the persistence with which such color and such shape appear together. The true being of the horse is behind its apparent, visible, and tangible elements. It is a thing which is latent under those present things—color, shape, and so on. A thing, then, which is thought of as a unitary support for those other things which I call "the qualities of the horse"—not, properly speaking, the "horse" itself. Therefore, the being of this animal is not its visible and apparent being, but on the contrary, something in it which supports its appearances, its substratum being made up of qualities, the being which is underneath or behind them, their substantial being, their substance. Substance, then, is a thing I assume to be behind what I see of the thing, of its appearance.

But in addition the horse moves, changes the color of his skin with the years and even changes his shape with work—therefore his appearances are infinite. If the horse were to consist of his appearances, he would be not one horse, but an infinite number of horses, all different. That is to say, the horse would be this and that and the other, and therefore, neither this nor that nor anything specific and determined. But let us suppose that under those appearances there is a thing which is invisible and permanent, which produces those appearances one after another. Then we can say that they are changes in one single, unique being: the substance called "horse." While the same horse may shift in shape, bulk and color, while he changes in appearance, he has in reality a being which is both quiet and immutable. The substance, in addition to being the support of his various qualities, is the permanent subject of their accidents or their variations.

The most characteristic expression of the Hellenic concept of being is the underlying, essential, or substantial being, the being which is immovable and unchanging. Included in the ultimate substance, the beginning of all change and movement, we shall find in the Aristotelian God a being which moves other beings but is itself moved by nothing, a motor force which is immobile, χινοῦν ἀχίνητον. This idea of a being at once substantive and static is most just, and indestructible if there are no other realities in the world than those that reach us from afar, those we perceive. Because the fact is that of those external things we have only their appearance. But the horse does not exist solely for the reason that he appears; indeed, we say of this appearance that it is only appearance and not reality.

Try, for example, to consider pure color as a reality, as something which in the process of being sustains itself and is sufficient unto itself. You will note that this is as impossible as it would be to have an inverse without a reverse, an upper without a lower. Color reveals itself as a fragment of a reality which completes it, of a material which at once adorns it and upholds it. So one postulates the reality which allows it to exist and as long as we neither find it nor assume it, this does not seem to us to have reached its true and definite being. I mentioned this earlier, and used it because it is the most traditional and most famous example, the thing with which one must begin in order to go on making oneself understood. That is, like so many things in this course which seem so well known, I said it then so that I could unsay it later.

This is why Descartes, when he sees that thought consists in the appearance of itself to itself, does not believe that it is sufficient unto itself; he then applies to it blindly, almost mechanically, the old category of substance and seeks beneath thought an underlying, a substantive thing which gives it forth and which in it is made manifest. Thus it seems to him that he has found the essence, the being of thought not in thought itself, but in a thing— a thing which thinks, a *res cogitans*. For him it is the substance *quod nihil aliud indigeat ad existendum.* So that on the one hand, thought is the only thing which indubitably exists because in order to be itself it needs only to appear; and on the other, in order to exist it must have this underlying and non-appearing support—a thing which thinks. Do you not see that we are following the idea of the *iman*, the magnet, the magic habit of assuming that behind what we see there is something which explains the apparent, an entity which we do not see and which is itself a mystery?

In point of fact, no one ever has had an intuition of a substance. Descartes replaces the first part of his phrase, which is obvious—that thought exists—by the second, which is highly problematical, useless, and which devitalizes thought's manner of being by solidifying it and paralyzing it into a substantive being, a thing. No; the thought and the self are not one and the same thing. Thought, in order to exist, needs nothing; otherwise Descartes could not have accepted the first part of his phrase, could not have said *cogito*—thought exists—and have founded on that truth his conclusion—*hence*, I exist.

One must recognize that this Cartesian formula—infused with genius though it is and most fruitful for the whole sector of seminal truth which, despite itself, it drags behind it—is in detail and in the whole a tangle of contradictions. Therefore hardly anyone in the three centuries of its existence has properly understood it. And you may be sure that those few who have managed truly to understand it have done so only because they had the courage to be sincere with themselves and to recognize that in the beginning they did not understand it.

For three years I lived in a German town where they call themselves specialists in Cartesian thought. I put myself docilely under that discipline, day after day and month after month—yet I assure you that in Marburg they have never understood the Descartes formula, the root of that idealism which is the philosophy that Marburg pretended to cultivate. And the prevailing state of sterility came from what is an almost constant ailment of the intelligent; they try more or less violently to extract a meaning from a phrase, and this they call understanding it. In order truly to understand it one must ask oneself if this is the only meaning which the phrase holds, that is to say, the only one corresponding to the phrase in its entirety. The "*cogito, sum*" *can* say many things, an infinite number of things—but in truth it says one thing only, and it is this which it is important to understand.

Descartes turns the subject of thought into substance, and in so doing, tosses it outside of thought; he converts it to a cosmic and external thing, in that it no longer consists in being thought, and only insofar as it is thought is it within itself, making itself and giving being to itself. The thinking *thing* does not think about itself—as the substance "stone" or "house" does not consist in seeming to itself a "house" or a "stone." Well now, I am nothing but what I seem to myself to be, basically and across the board. All the rest is magic.

Idealism's inability to invent a new manner of being which would permit it complete fidelity to its thesis appears no less clearly if we pass from the subject of the thought to the object. Idealism proposes to me that I suspend my belief in the reality which this theatre seems to have outside my mind. It says to me, that this theatre is in truth only a thought, a vision or an image of this theatre. Hence it becomes the same as that chimera of which we were talking the other day and which we classed as an imaginary being, thus taking it out of the real garden and putting it into the fountain, that is to say, into the mind. For the moment, things are no more than "contents of the conscious." This is the phrase which the nineteenth century used most often in philosophy; it is not in Descartes although it could and should be there, but it germinates in the books of Kant. Thanks to him we take external reality and put it within the mind.

But let us go softly. Let us see what in this fundamental thesis of idealism is firm and what is inacceptable. It is certain that the presumed external reality of the world is only a presumption; that is to say, a reality in itself and independent of me is highly problematical. Therefore philosophy cannot accept it. What does this mean? Simply that the external world is not really outside my acquiring an understanding of it, that the outside world exists not in the outside world but within my recognition of it. Where shall we put it, then? Within my recognition of it, my mind, my thought, within me. Idealism sees the question as a dilemma; either this theatre has an absolute reality outside of me, or within me; in order to be, it must stand somewhere, and there is no doubt that it is a thing. I cannot give assurance that it is outside of me for the reason that I cannot emerge from myself in order to go forth to that pretended absolute reality which is outside myself. So there is no alternative but to recognize its existence as a mental content within myself.

But idealism ought to move with more caution. Before resolving that there are no more than those two possibilities—either within me or outside of me—it should meditate quietly on the following: Has the expression, "content of the conscious," or "mental content" any intelligible meaning when it is said about this theatre? Or is it rather a bit of nonsense, a combination of words as repugnant to each other as "squared circle"?

Let us look at it. What do I mean when I use the phrase, "this theatre"? By "this theatre," I understand a room twenty meters high or more, with a certain breadth and length, containing blue chairs, a set of flies and backdrops, and so on. If I say that this is the content of my conscious self, I am saying that something twenty meters in height blue in color, etc., forms an effective part of me. But if it forms a part of me, I can say that, at least in part, my self, my thought, is so many feet high by so many feet broad; consequently that I am extensive, that my thought occupies space and that it has in it a piece of something blue.

The absurdity of this becomes quickly apparent, and the idealist defends himself by saying, "I withdraw the expression, 'theatre-content of the conscious self,' and in place of it I will say, 'that which is contained within my thought, my consciousness is, of course, only my thinking about the theatre, the image of it, or my imagining this theatre.'" There is no inconvenience in that I am thinking, I am imagining, there is nothing strange in the idea that my thinking, my imagining, should form part of me, or should be contained within me. But in that case we are not talking about the theatre; we have left the theatre outside. So it is false to say that it is either within or without. The theatre, the external reality, always remains outside of me, it is not within me. The world is not my representation—in this phrase of Schopenhauer, as in almost all of idealism, the words are used with a double meaning. I represent the world to myself. What is mine is the act of representing, and this is what representation clearly means.

But the world which I represent to myself is not my representing, but the thing which is represented. My part is the representing, not the represented. Schopenhauer makes the primary error of confusing in the single word, "representation," the two terms whose relationship he sets out to discuss, the thinking and the thing which is thought. Here is the decisive reason why I described that famous phrase, the title of his amusing book, as rough, uncouth, unpolished. It is more than rough; a boy would call it woolly.

Where, then, is the theatre in any definitive sense? The reply is obvious; it is not inside my thought and forming part of it, but neither is it outside my thought if by outside one understands having nothing to do with it—it is inseparably linked with my thinking of it, neither outside my thought nor within it, but linked with it; as is inverse with reverse, left with right; yet right is not left nor is reverse the same as inverse.

Remember the type of reasoning we were doing when we followed idealism until we reached its thesis. I see the garden, I close my eyes, and I cease to see it. This is beyond dispute. What has happened here? The garden and my seeing of it have come to an end at one and the same time—my consciousness and its object, my thinking, and that which is thought of. But when I open my eyes again, the garden reappears—hence insofar as thought and seeing begin to exist, so does their object, the thing seen. This is the indisputable fact. And as philosophy aspires to be composed only of indisputable facts, one need only take things as they are and say: the external world does not exist except in my thinking of it, but the external world is not my thought; I am neither the theatre nor the world—I am confronting this theatre, I am linked with the world—together we are the world and I. And generalizing, we will say: the world is not a reality subsisting in itself and independent of me—it is what it is *for* me, and for the moment it is nothing more.

Up to this point we march step by step with idealism. But we are adding things: as the world is only what it seems to me that it is, it will be only an apparent being, and there is no reason that obliges me to seek for it a substance which is beyond that appearance—I need neither hunt for it in a supporting cosmos as did the ancients, nor make out of myself a substance which carries with it, as content and representation, the things which I see and touch, smell and imagine. This is the great ancient prejudice which modern ideology ought to eliminate.

This theatre and I confront one another with no intermediary between us; the theatre exists because I see it, and it is just what I see of it, as I see it; it exhausts its being in its appearance. But it is not within me, nor is it confused with me; our relations are clear and unequivocal. I am the one who now sees it, it is what I now see, without it and other things like it, my seeing would not exist, that is to say, I would not exist. Without objects there is no subject.

Idealism's error was to convert itself into subjectivism, by emphasizing the dependence of things on the one who thinks of them, their dependence on my subjectivity, without noticing at the same time that my subjectivity also depends on the existence of objects. The error lay in making me swallow the world, in place of leaving us both inseparable, immediate and together, but at the same time distinct and different. As a *quid pro quo* it would be as ridiculous to say that I am blue because I see blue objects as it is to say that the blue object is part of my being, of myself, because it is seen by me. I am always with myself, I am no other than what I think I am, I cannot go out of myself—but in order to find a world which is distinct from me I do not need to go out of myself; the world is always linked with me and my being is a being with the world. I am my innermost being, for no transcendent being enters into me, but at the same time I am a place where the world appears naked; it is the thing I am not, the exotic in me. The outside world, the cosmos, is immediate to me, and in this sense is intimate, but it is not I, and in this sense it is alien and strange to me.

We need, then, to correct philosophy's point of departure. The basic datum of the Universe is not simply that either thought exists or I, the thinker, exist, but that if thought exists, *ipso facto,* I who think and the world about which I think also exist; the one exists with the other, having no possible separation between them. I am not a substantial being nor is the world, but we both are in active correlation; I am that which sees the world and the world is that which is seen by me. I exist for the world, and the world exists for me. If there were no things to be seen, thought about, and imagined, I would not see, think, or imagine; that is to say, I would not exist.

In one corner of Leibnitz' work, where he makes a quick criticism of his predecessor Descartes, he notes that in his judgment there is no one single first truth about the Universe, but two which are equally and inseparably foremost: one of these reads, *sum cogitans,* I exist as thinking, and the other says, *plura a me cogitantur*—many things are thought by me. It is surprising that up to now no one has profited by this great mental discovery, not even through Leibnitz.

In short, on searching carefully for the basic data of

the Universe—which undoubtedly exist in the Universe
—and on exaggerating the factor of doubt, I find that
there is one primary and fundamental fact which carries
its own assurance. This fact is the joint existence of a
self, a subjectivity, and of its world. The one does not
exist without the other. I acquire no understanding of
myself except as I take account of objects, of the surroundings. I do not think unless I think of things—therefore on finding myself I always find a world confronting
me. Insofar as subjectivity and thought are concerned, I
find myself as part of a dual fact whose other part is a
world. Therefore the basic and undeniable fact is not my
existence, but my coexistence with the world.

The tragedy of idealism stems from the fact that having transmuted the world as an alchemist might, into
"subject," into the content of subject, it enclosed this
subject within itself; then there was no way of explain-
ing clearly how, if this theatre is only my image and a
piece of me, it appears to be so completely different
from me. But now we have won through to an entirely
different situation; we have stumbled on the fact that
that which cannot be doubted is a relation between two
inseparable terms. The one who thinks, who acquires
understanding, and the other which is understood. The
conscious self goes on being the innermost self, but now
I become close and intimate not only with my subjectivity, but also with my objectivity, with the world
which is clear and simple before me. The conscious self
is not a recluse, but on the contrary, is that most strange
primary reality assumed in every other reality, which
consists in the fact that someone, I, am myself precisely
when I am taking account of things, of the world. This
is the sovereign peculiarity of the mind which must be
accepted, recognized, and beautifully described just as

it is, in all its marvelous strangeness. Far from the self being closed, it is *par excellence* the open being. To see this theatre is to open myself to what I am not.

This new situation is not paradoxical; it coincides with the native attitude of the mind, conserves it and recognizes its good sense. But it also does something else; out of the realist thesis which serves as the base for ancient philosophy, it saves that part which is essential: namely, that the external world is not illusion, not hallucination, not a subjective world. And all this the new position achieves by insisting on and purifying the idealist thesis whose decisive affirmation consists in noting that the only thing which indubitably exists is what appears to me to exist. Do you see how the daughter ideas, the truly novel ones, bear in their wombs their mothers, the truly old ones, the true and fruitful old ones?

Let us repeat—all surpassing is conserving. It is not true that basically only the conscious self exists, only thinking, only the I. The truth is that I exist with my world and in my world—and I consist in occupying myself with this my world, in seeing it, imagining it, thinking about it, loving it, hating it, being sad or being happy in it and through it, in moving about in it, in transforming it and in suffering from it. Nothing of this could I do if the world did not coexist with me, if it were not confronting me, surrounding me, pressing at me, manifesting itself, creating enthusiasm in me, afflicting me.

But what is this? What have we unwittingly stumbled upon? The basic fact of someone who sees and loves and hates and desires a world, and who moves within it, suffers for it, and in it exerts himself—this is what has always, in the humblest and most universal words been called "my life." What is this? It is simply that the primordial reality, the fact of all facts, the datum for the Universe, that which is given to me is . . . "my life"—not myself alone, not my hermetic conscious self; these things are interpretations, the idealist interpretations. "My life" is given to me, and my life is primarily a finding of myself in the world: nor is there vagueness in this. I am in this very world, the world of now; here in this theatre which is a bit of my vital world, here at this instant, doing what I am doing in it. I am philosophizing.

Abstractions are finished. When I seek the indubitable fact, I do not find the generic thing which is thought, but the highly personal self—I who am thinking of the basic thing, I who am now philosophizing. This is how the first thing that philosophy meets is the fact of a person who philosophizes, who wants to think about the Universe and to that end seeks something which cannot be doubted.

But note well that what it finds is not a philosophic theory but the philosopher in the act of philosophizing, that is to say, in the act of living the process of philosophizing, just as this same philosopher might later be found wandering in a fit of melancholy through the streets, dancing in a nightclub, suffering indigestion, or smitten with a passing beauty. That is to say, he finds philosophizing, theorizing, to be a vital act, a vital fact; it is a detail of his life and within his life, that life which is enormous, gay and sad, hopeful and frightening.

So the first thing that philosophy must do is to define that datum, to define "my life," "our life," the life of every one of us. To live is the process of going down to the roots: Every other thing, every other manner of being I find within my own life, both as a detail of it and with reference to it. In it is all the rest, and all the rest is what it is with regard to that life. The most abstruse mathematical equation, the most abstract and solemn philosophic concept, the very Universe, even God himself, are things that I find in my life, things that I live. And the basic and primary being of these things is, therefore, that of being lived by me, and I cannot define what they are in terms of being lived until I find out what it is "to live."

Biologists use the word "life" in order to designate the phenomena of organic beings. The organic is only one class of things that are found in life, together with another class of things called inorganic. What the philosopher tells us about organisms is important, but it is also evident that when we say we live, and talk about "our life," the life of every one of us, we give this word a meaning which is more immediate, broader and more decisive. The savage and the ignorant man are not acquainted with biology, yet they have a right to talk of "their lives," and to have us understand that beneath this term lies an enormous fact, predating all biology, all science, all culture—the magnificent, fundamental, and frightening fact which is assumed and implied by all the other facts. The biologist finds "organic life" within his own life, as a detail of that life: it is one of his vital occupations and nothing more. Biology, like every science, is an activity or a form of going on living. Philosophy is, first of all, philosophizing, and philosophizing is undoubtedly a way of living—as is running, falling in love, playing golf, growing indignant in politics, and being a lady in society. They are all of them forms and ways of living.

Therefore the basic problem of philosophy is to define that way of being, that primary problem which we call "our life." Well, now, living is something that no one can do for me—life is not transferable—it is not an abstract concept, it is my most individual being. For the first time philosophy has a point of departure which is not an abstraction.

This is the new landscape which I was announcing, the oldest of all, the one we have always been setting aside, been leaving behind us. In order to begin, philosophy goes behind itself, sees itself as a form of life, which is what it truly and concretely is: in short, it takes shelter in life, submerges itself in life, and for the moment it is meditation on our life. So old a landscape is this which appears so new. So new that it is the enormous discovery of our time. So new is it that none of the concepts of traditional philosophy are of any use in it: that way of being which is living requires new categories, not the categories of the ancient cosmic beings—one tries to escape from them and to find the categories of living, the essence of "our life."

Now you will see how everything which may have seemed to you difficult to understand, impalpable, spectral, a mere play on words, reappears as something clear, straightforward, and as though you had been thinking it any number of times. So clear, so straight, so evident that at times it will seem too much so, and on hearing it—I ask pardon for this in advance—on hearing it, you are going to be disturbed because we are going inevitably to touch the secret of the life of every one of you. Let us reveal a secret. Life is a secret.

10

A New Reality and a New Idea
of Reality. The Indigent Self. To
Live Is to Find Ourselves in the
World. To Live Is to Decide What
We are Going to Be.

IN the previous chapter we found as a fundamental datum
of the Universe (hence a primordial reality) something
which is completely new, something very different from
the cosmic being with which the ancients started, and
also different from the subjective being with which the
moderns started.

This statement that we have found a new reality, a
new being hitherto unknown, may not convey to all of
you the full significance of those words. You think that
at most this is a new thing, different from known things,
but in the last analysis a "thing," like all the other things
—you assume that this concerns a being or a reality
which, though different from other beings and realities
already well known, still fits with what the words "being" and "reality" have always meant—in short, that the
discovery, however important, is of the same kind as if
one were discovering a new animal in zoology, which
might be new, but is neither more nor less an animal than
those which are already known, so that the concept

"animal" still has value for it.

I am very sorry to tell you that what we have been discussing is far more important and decisive than that. We have found a new basic reality, therefore something radically different from what has been known and recognized in philosophy, therefore something for which the traditional concepts of reality and of being do not serve. If, notwithstanding this, we go on using them, it is because until this new reality was discovered, we had no concepts of which we could make use other than the old ones. In order to formulate a new concept we must first have something which is completely novel. The result of this is that the find becomes, not only a new reality, but the beginning of a new idea of being, of a new science of being, of a new philosophy, and in the measure in which this influences life, of a whole new life, a *vita nova.*

It is not yet possible for the most brilliant to give a clear account of the projections and perspectives which that discovery contains for the present and will involve for the future. Nor do I urge it. I need not appraise today the importance of what was said previously—I am in no hurry to give reasons. Reason is not a train leaving at a fixed hour. The only ones in a hurry are the sick and the ambitious. All I desire is that among the young who listen to me there may be some with souls which are profoundly masculine and therefore very sensitive to adventures of the intellect, who will inscribe what I said last Friday in their fresh memories, and in the fullness of time will generously remember them.

For the ancients, reality, being, meant a "thing"; for the moderns, being meant "innermost, subjectivity"; for us, being means "living," therefore intimacy with ourselves and with things. We can be sure that we have reached a higher spiritual level because if we look down at our feet, at our point of departure which is "living," we find that in it the ancient and the modern are conserved, integrated one with another, and superseded. We are at a higher level, we are at our own level, we are at the level of the times. The concept of level of the times is not a mere phrase. As we shall soon see, it is a reality.

Let us briefly retrace the path which has led us to the point where we come to "living" as the basic datum, the primordial and indubitable reality of the Universe. The existence of things, like my own independent existence, is problematical; in consequence we abandon the realist thesis of the ancients. On the other hand, the fact that I think about things cannot be doubted, nor can it be doubted that my thought exists, and that therefore the existence of things is dependent on me, is a matter of my thinking them; this is the solid portion of the idealist thesis. For that we accept it, but in order to accept it we want to understand it well, and we ask ourselves, in what sense and what manner do things depend on me when I think them—what *are* things, themselves, when I say that they are only my thoughts?

Idealism answers that things depend on me, are thoughts, in the sense that they are contents of my consciousness, of my thinking, states of my self. This is the second part of the idealist thesis and it is this that we do not accept. And we do not accept it for the reason that it is nonsense. Not because it is not true, but for a more elemental reason. In order for a phrase to be not true it must have some sense, some meaning; it is for the very reason that we understand the meaning of "two and two make five" that we say it is not true.

But that second part of the idealist thesis has no meaning; like the "squared circle," it is a piece of nonsense. As long as this theatre is this theatre, it cannot be something contained within my self. My self is neither extensive nor blue, and this theatre is both extensive and blue. What I contain and what I am is only my seeing the theatre or thinking about it, my seeing or thinking of the star, but it is not the theatre itself or the star itself. The relationship between thinking and the objects of that thinking cannot be, as the idealist pretended, a matter of having them within me, as though they were ingredients of me; on the contrary, it is a matter of my finding them different from and outside of myself.

So it is false to think that the conscious self is closed, that it recognizes only itself, only what it has within. On the contrary, I am aware of what I am thinking when, for example, I take account of what I see or think about a star; what I then recognize is that two different things exist, though they are joined one to the other—I who see the star, and the star which is seen by me. The star needs me, but also I need the star. If idealism were to say no more than this—that thought, the subject, the self, exists —it would be saying something that, though incomplete, would be true, but it is not content with this. It adds that *only* thought, the subject, the self, exists. This is false. If the subject exists, so does the object, inseparably and vice versa. If I who think exist, so also does the world of which I am thinking. Therefore, the fundamental, the radical truth is the coexistence of myself with the world. Existing is first and foremost coexisting—it is I myself seeing something which is not myself, it is I loving another being, it is I suffering from things.

The form of relationship by which things are mine is not, then, the unilateral dependence which idealism believed it had found; it is not only that they are what I think and feel them to be, but also that there is an inverse dependence, also I depend on them, on the world. What we are talking of is an interdependence, a correlation, in short, a coexistence.

Why did idealism, which had so clear and strong an intuition of thought, conceive it so badly as to falsify it? For the simple reason that it accepted the traditional meaning of the concept of being and existing without discussing it. According to this very old meaning, to be, to exist, implies complete independence—hence, for the philosophic past, the only true being is the Absolute Being, which represents the superlative of ontological independence. More clearly than anyone before him, and almost cynically, did Descartes formulate this idea of being at the same time as he defined substance, saying (as I said before) that it is *"quod nihil aliud indigeat ad existendum."* The being which, in order to be, needs nothing else, *nihil indigeat.* The substantive being is the independent being, sufficient unto itself. When idealism trips over the obvious fact that the fundamental and indubitable reality is the fact that I think, and the thing that I think (hence a duality and a correlation), it does not dare to conceive it impartially, but says, "granted that I find these two things—the subject and the object—united and therefore dependent one on the other, I must decide which of the two is independent, which does not need the other, which is the sufficient one." But we do not find any indubitable basis for the assumption that "being" can mean only "self-sufficient being." On the contrary, the only indubitable being which we find is the interdependence between things and the self—things are what they are to me, and I am what suffers from things—therefore the indubitable being is for the moment not the sufficient being but the "needy being." It is a mutual need which defines beings. To be is to need; I need things, things need me.

This modification is of extraordinary importance, but it is so much a matter of surface, so far from profound, so clear, so simple that one is almost ashamed of it. Do you see how philosophy is a constant will toward superficiality? A game which involves turning the cards so that the opponent can see them?

The basic fact, we were saying, is the coexistence of myself with things. But scarcely have we said that when we perceive that to call the manner in which I exist with the world, that primary reality, at once unitary and dual, that magnificent fact of essential duality—to call all that "coexistence" is to commit an error. For coexistence means only that one thing stands beside another, that the one and the other have being. What we are trying to express is rendered false by the prone and static character of those two old concepts, being and existing. This is not merely a matter of the world being by itself, next to me, and I for my part being here, next to the world, but a concept that the world is what it continues to be because of me, that its character is dynamic, confronting me, opposing me; and I am the one who acts upon it, who looks at it, dreams it, suffers it, loves it and detests it.

The static concept of being can be declared done and finished—later we will see what its subordinate role becomes—and for it there must be substituted an active being. The world's being as it confronts me is, we might say, a matter of functioning with respect to me, and similarly of my acting toward it. But this—a reality consisting of a self which sees the world, thinks about it, touches it, loves it or detests it, is enthusiastic about it or irritated at it, transforms it, exhausts it, suffers it— this is what has always been called "living." This is "my life," "our life," the life of every one of us.

Let us, then, wring the necks of those venerable and consecrated words, "existing," "coexisting," "being," and in place of them say that the primary thing in the Universe is "my living" and whatever else is there or not, within the compass of my life. Now there is no awkwardness in saying that things, the Universe, God Himself, are contained within my life, because "my life" is not myself alone, not only the subject I; my living includes the world. We have moved past three centuries of subjectivism—the self has been freed from its internal prison, it is no longer the only thing there is, no longer does it suffer that solitude which we met earlier, that comes with being the one and only. We have escaped from that tendency toward retiring within oneself from which we suffer as moderns, that shadowy confinement without light from the outside world, without space in which to free the wings of eagerness and appetite. We are outside the narrow cell of the self, outside the hermit's sick room lined with mirrors which returned to us only our own image, outside in the free air, lungs once more open to cosmic oxygen, wings lifted for flight, hearts aimed toward kindness. Once again the world becomes that vital horizon which curves about us like the line of the sea, the magnificent bend of its bow inspiring our hearts with a yearning for the arrow—that heart which, sanguine in itself, is always being pierced with pain or with delight. Let us save ourselves in the world, "save ourselves in things."

I wrote that last phrase as a program for life when, at the age of twenty-two, I was studying in the Mecca of idealism and trembling with anticipation of the cloudy coming of a future maturity. *E quindi uscimmo a riveder le stelle.*

But first we must find out what, in its own peculiar

way, is that true and primary being which is "living." In this attempt, none of the concepts and categories of traditional philosophy are of any use to us. What we are now seeing is new: we must therefore conceive what we see with concepts that are novices. We have the good fortune to present concepts in their first appearance on the stage. In our present situation we can well understand the delight which the Greeks must have felt. They were the first men to discover scientific thinking and theory —that most special and ingenious caress which the mind gives to things, molding itself to them in an exact idea. The Greeks had no scientific past at their backs, they received no ready-made concepts nor technical words which must be held sacred. They had before them the being which they had discovered and they had at hand only the current language—"the master tongue in which each man talks with his neighbor"—and suddenly one of the homely everyday words slides wonderfully into place to describe precisely that most important reality which they had before them. The humble word ascended, as by levitation, from the vulgar plane of gossip, of daily chatter, and was raised nobly to the status of a technical term, rising proud as a palfrey with the weight of the sovereign idea loaded on its back. When a new world is discovered, the needed words are fortunate. We ourselves, heirs of a very profound past, seem condemned to manipulate within the sciences only hieratical terms, solemn and rigid; having too long respected them, we have lost all confidence in them.

What a pleasure it must have been for those men of Greece to be present at the moment in which the Pentecost of the scientific idea descended like a sublime flame over the most trivial word! Think how hard, rigid, inert, cold as metal, the word "hypotenuse" must have sounded to the ear of a child who heard it for the first time! One fine day, there beside the Greek sea, some intelligent musicians called Pythagoreans discovered that in the harp there was a proportion between the length of the longest and shortest strings which agreed with the proportion between the sounds made by the two. The harp is a triangle closed by a cord—"the longest and most extended"—in other words, a hypotenuse. Who today could feel in that horrible word with its masked face that simple and sweet meaning, "the longest," which recalls the title of Debussy's waltz "La plus que lente"?

Well, then, we find ourselves in a similar situation. We search for concepts and categories which say, "to live," in all its aspects, we need to plunge our hands down into the simplest vocabulary and to surprise ourselves with the fact that suddenly a word with no special standing, with no scientific past, a poor, everyday word, can suddenly be lit from within by the light of a scientific idea and converted into a technical term. This is one more sign of the way fortune has favored us; we arrive fresh and new on an unspoiled coast.

The word "to live" does no more than bring us close to the wordless abyss that lies masked and hidden beyond that coast. We must have courage to put foot into that abyss even though we know we face perilous immersion and frightening depths. There are beneficent chasms which, out of their pure and unsoundable depths, return us to the surface of existence, leaving us restored, robust and illumined. There are fundamental facts which need to be looked at from time to time for the very reason that they are abysmal, and we lose ourselves in them. Jesus said it divinely: "Only he who loses himself shall find himself." If you will follow me with extra attention, we will for a moment lose ourselves. We are going to dive deep into our own existence so that we may come to the surface like the Coromandel fisherman who rises from the bottom of the sea with the pearl between his teeth, and therefore smiling.

What is our life, my life? It would be naive, and out of order, to answer this question with biological definitions or to talk of cells, somatic functions, digestion, the nervous system, and so on. All these things are hypothetical realities with a good basis, built up by the science of biology, which is merely one activity in my life when I study it or when I dedicate myself to its investigations. My life is not what happens in my cells any more than what happens in my stars, in those tiny golden points that I see in my night-time world. My very body is no more than a detail of the world which I find within myself— a detail which for many reasons is of exceptional importance to me, but which does not thereby shed the character of being only one ingredient among any number of others in the world about me. However much is said to me about my bodily organism, and whatever is added by psychology concerning my psychic organism, these refer to secondary peculiarities which assume the fact that I live and that in living I meet, see, analyze and investigate both the body-things and the soul-things. Consequently, replies of that kind are not even tangential to the primordial reality which we are now trying to define.

What, then, is life? Do not search afar, do not try to remember bits of wisdom learned from others. Fundamental truths must always be close at hand because only the close kind are fundamental. Those that must be searched for are the ones which are the private truths, local truths, provincial truths, isolated truths, but not basic truths. Life is what we are and what we do; it is therefore made up of all the things that are nearest to each one of us. Reach out a hand for it, and it will let itself be caught like a tame bird.

If, on coming here a moment ago, someone asked you where you were going, you would have said, "We are going to hear a lecture on philosophy." And here you are, in fact, listening to me. This has no particular importance. Nevertheless, it is what now makes up your life. I am sorry for you, but truth obliges me to say that your life, your now, consists of something of such minuscule importance. But if we are sincere, we will recognize that the greater part of our existence is made up of similar insignificances: we come, we go, we do this or that or the other, we think, we want or we do not want, and so on. From time to time our lives seem to take on a sudden tension, as if rising to their full height, becoming concentrated: it is some great sorrow, some great desire which calls us: we say that important things are happening to us. But note that so far as our lives are concerned, this variety of accents, this being important or not, makes no difference, for the critical and frenetic hour is no more and no less a matter of life than the throng of minutes that are commonplace and habitual.

So our first glance at life in this search for its pure essence yields us the group of acts and events which continue to provide what we might call its furnishings.

Our method will consist in noting the attributes of our life, one after another, in moving from those which are most external to those which lie deepest within us, so that from the periphery of living we withdraw to its throbbing center. We will find, then, an inward-moving series of definitions of life, each one of which conserves and adds depth to those that precede it.

The first one is this:

To live is what we do and what happens to us—from thinking or dreaming or being emotionally stirred, to playing the stock market or winning battles. But of course, nothing of what we do would be our life if we failed to recognize it as such. This is the first decisive attribute which we find: living is that strange, that unique and magical reality which has the privilege of existing for itself. All living is one's own living, feeling oneself live, knowing oneself to be existing—where knowing implies no intellectual knowledge nor special wisdom, but is that surprising presence which one's own life has for every one of us: without that kind of knowing, without that recognition of itself, the aching tooth would not hurt us.

The stone does not feel itself a stone, nor does it know that it is a stone: concerning itself, as everything else, it is completely blind. On the other hand, living is for the moment a revelation, a refusal to rest content with sheer being unless one sees or understands what one is, a process of inquiry, of informing oneself about oneself. It is the incessant discovery of ourselves and the world around us. Now we are come to the explanation of that strange possessive which we use when we say, "our life"; it is *ours* because in addition to being ours, we recognize that it is so, and that it is of this kind or that. On perceiving ourselves, we take possession of ourselves, and this finding oneself always in possession of oneself, this basic and perpetual being present at whatever we do and are, is what differentiates living from everything else. Proud science, learned knowledge, does no more than take advantage of, particularize, and regiment this primary revelation of which life consists.

As an image which will help to fix this idea in your memories, let us cite that incident of Egyptian mythology in which Osiris dies, and Isis, his beloved, eager to bring

him back to life, makes him swallow the eye of the
falcon, Horus. From then on the eye appears in all the
hieratical drawings of Egyptian civilization, representing
the first attribute of life—the act of seeing oneself. And
that eye, traveling throughout the whole Mediterranean,
filling the Orient with its influence, has been painted by
all the rest of the religions as the first attribute of Provi-
dence, the seeing of oneself, the first essential attribute of
life itself.

This seeing, this being aware of oneself, this presence
of my life before me which gives me possession of it,
which makes it "mine," is what the mindless lack. The
madman's life is not his own; strictly speaking, it is no
longer a life. Hence it is one of the most disturbing things
in the world to see a madman. Because the physiognomy
of a life appears perfect in him, but only as a mask behind which life itself is absent. Facing a demented man
we feel as though facing a mask; he is the essential and
definitive mask. Not knowing himself, the madman does
not belong to himself, he has been expropriated, and ex-
propriation, passing into alien possession, is what the old
phrases about madness meant: "absent-minded," "insane,"
we say, "he is beside himself," he is "gone" from himself,
he is "possessed," which is to say, he is possessed by another. Life is knowing oneself, it is evidential.

It is right to say that living comes first and then philosophizing—in a very strict sense this is, as you see, the
principle of my entire philosophy. It is well that this
should be said, but not without noting that the root and
heart of living consists of knowing oneself and understanding oneself, of observing oneself and what surrounds
one, of being transparent to oneself. Therefore, when we
put the question, "What is our life?" we might answer,
"Life is what we do, of course, because living is know-

ing what we do; in short, it is finding oneself in the
world and being occupied with the things and beings in
the world."

These common words—*finding oneself, world, being
occupied*—are now technical words in this new philosophy. One could talk a long time about every one of
them, but I will limit myself to observing that this definition, "to live is to find oneself in a world," like all the
principal ideas in these lectures, can be found elsewhere
in my published work. It is important to me to mention
this, especially with regard to the idea of existence, for
which I claim ideological priority. For that very reason,
I am glad to recognize that the man who has gone deepest
into the analysis of life is the German philosopher, Martin
Heidegger.

Here we must sharpen our vision a bit, for we are approaching a more perilous shoreline.

To live is to find oneself amid the world. In a recent
work of genius, Heidegger has made us note the enormous
significance of those words. This is not chiefly a matter
of finding our own body among other corporeal things
and finding these things within a great space or body
which we would call the world. If there were only
bodies, the process of living would not exist, but bodies
would roll about, one against another, separate as billiard
balls or atoms, without any of them knowing or caring
about any of the others. The world in which we find ourselves living is composed of some things which are agreeable and others which are disagreeable, of the atrocious
and the benevolent, the pleasant and the perilous; the
important thing is not whether things are or are not
bodies, but that they affect us, interest us, caress us,
threaten us and torment us. Originally, what we call a
body is only something that either resists us and obstructs

us, or upholds us and sustains us; therefore it is something either favorable to us or unfavorable. *Sensu stricto*, the world is what affects us. And living means that each one finds himself in a range of themes and subjects which affect him. Thus, without knowing how it happens, life finds itself at the same time that it discovers the world. There is no living except in a world full of other things, whether they be objects or creatures; it is seeing things and places, loving them or hating them, desiring them or fearing them. All living is busying oneself with another thing which is not oneself, all living is living together with one's surroundings.

Accordingly, our life is not only our person, but part of it is our world. Our life is made up of our person busying itself with things; what our life is obviously depends as much on what our person is as on what our world is. Therefore we can picture "our life" as an arc which unites the world and the self; but as between the world and the self there is no priority; neither comes first, but both come at the same time. Nor is the one or the other nearer us; we do not first take account of ourselves and then of what lies about us, but living is finding oneself face to face with the world, inside the world, submerged in its drudgery, in its problems, in its unhappy complications. But by the same token it is also the opposite; that world, being composed only of what affects each one of us, is inseparable from us. We are born with it close to us, and we are as vitally person and world as those pairs of divinities of ancient Greece or Rome which were born and lived together—the Dioscuros, for example, pairs of gods which used to be called *dii consentes*, the unanimous gods.

We live here, now—that is to say, we find ourselves in one place in the world and it seems to us that we have

come here of our own free will. As a matter of fact, life
leaves a fair margin of possibilities within the world, but
we are not free to be or not to be in this present world.
It is possible to renounce life, but if one goes on living
one cannot choose the world in which one lives. This
gives to life a face which is terribly dramatic. To live is
not to enter by choice into a place which has been chosen
earlier according to one's taste, as one might choose a
theatre after dinner; it is to find oneself suddenly fallen,
submerged, projected without knowing how, into a
world which cannot be changed, into the world of now.
Our life begins with the astonishing and continuous surprise of existence. Without our previous consent, we are
shipwrecked in a world we neither built nor thought
about. We did not give ourselves life, but we find it at
the very moment when we find ourselves. Anyone carried
asleep to the wings of a theatre, and there thrust suddenly
and awake before the footlights and the public, would
be struck by a similar flash of illumination. When he finds
himself there, what is it that he finds? Without knowing
how or why he got there, he finds himself plunged into
a situation which is difficult; the difficult situation demands that he comport himself decently in that public
appearance which he neither sought, foresaw, nor prepared. Fundamentally, life is always unforeseen. No one
announced our appearance before we stepped onto its
stage—an always concrete and definite stage—no one
prepared us for it.

This sudden and unforeseen character is essential in
life. It would be very different if we could prepare ourselves before entering into it. Dante said that "the arrow
seen beforehand comes more slowly." But life is not an
arrow. As a whole, and in each of its moments, it has
about it more of a pistol shot fired at close range.

I think that this image paints with sufficient clarity the essence of living. Life is given to us—better, it is thrown at us, or we are thrown into it, but what it is that is given us, what life is—this is a problem that we must solve for ourselves. And it is a problem not only in those cases of especial difficulty which we describe as peculiarly full of woes and conflicts, but in all other cases. When you came here you had to decide to do it, to resolve to live for the moment in this manner. Or to put it another way, as we live we uphold ourselves in the air, balancing ourselves on a thin wire, carrying the weight of our lives above the crossroads of the world. And with this we do not prejudge whether our existence will be gay or sad: whichever it is, it is built out of an endless need for solving the problem of itself.

If the shot fired by the gun had a soul, it would feel that its trajectory was pre-fixed by the powder and the firing pin, and if we call this trajectory its life, the shot would be simply a spectator, with no way of intervening in it; the shot neither fired itself nor did it choose its target. But for this very reason, that kind of existence cannot be called life. Life is not felt as predetermined. However sure we may be as to what is going to happen tomorrow, we always see it as a possibility. This is another essential and dramatic attribute of our life to be added to the earlier one. For the same reason that it is continually a problem, big or little, which we must solve without any chance of passing it on to someone else, it is never a solved problem; at any moment we find ourselves forced to choose among various possibilities. If it is not given us to choose the world in which our life is to be unrolled—and this is the fateful dimension—we find ourselves with a certain margin, a vital horizon of possibilities, and this is the dimension of its liberty; this life is fate in freedom, and freedom in fate. Is this not surprising?

We have been tossed into our life, and at the same time we must, on our own account, construct that thing into which we have been tossed, we must fabricate it. Or to put it another way, our life is our being. We are whatever it is, and nothing more—but that being is not predetermined, nor resolved in advance; we must decide it ourselves, we must decide what we are going to be; for example, what we are going to be when we get ready to go forth from this theatre. This I call "raising oneself by the boot straps, upholding one's own being." There is neither rest nor pause because sleep, which is a biological form of living, does not exist for life in the basic sense in which we use this word. In slumber we do not live, but on awakening and renewing life we find it augmented by the fleeting memory of what we have dreamed.

The elemental and ancient metaphors are as true as Newton's laws. In those venerable metaphors which by now have become part of the language, over which we walk as on an island formed by what was once live coral —in these metaphors, I repeat, there live compressed the perfect intuitions of the most basic phenomena. Thus we frequently talk of suffering "under a heavy load," of finding ourselves in a "grave" situation. Weight and gravity are both transposed by metaphor from physical weight, from the bearing of another body on our own body, to the realm of spiritual worry. And in fact, life always does weigh on us, for it consists of carrying itself, supporting and directing itself. But nothing dulls the edge like habit, and ordinarily we forget this constant weight which we carry as part of us; the moment an unaccustomed problem presents itself, we feel the burden. While the star gravitates toward another body and does not weigh on itself, the living being is at one and the same time a weight which lies heavy and a hand which sustains. The word "joy" (in Spanish, *alegría*) is very close to "moving fleetly" (*aligerar*) which means to shed weight. The heavily burdened man goes to the tavern seeking joy—solid judgment slips away from him, and his life's poor aerostat rises joyously.

With all this we have taken notable steps in this vertical excursion, this descent into the profound depths of our life and our being. At this level, living appears to us as a process of feeling ourselves forced to decide what we are going to be. And we will not be content with saying, as we said in the beginning, that life is what we do, is a combining of our occupations with the things of the world, because we have noted that all that doing, all those occupations, do not come to us automatically; they are not mechanically imposed, like the songs on gramophone disks, but are decided by us; this fact of being decided is the living part of them—the execution is in large part mechanical.

The great fundamental fact which I want to bring you is here. We have put it into words: living is a constant process of deciding what we are going to do. Do you see the enormous paradox that is wrapped up in this? A being which consists not so much in what it is as in what it is going to be: therefore in what it has not yet become! This essential, this most profound paradox is our life. This is no fault of mine, but in solemn truth this is just what it is.

But perhaps some of you are now thinking, "So that is life—deciding what we are going to be! But we have been here for some time listening to him; we have been saying nothing, yet certainly we have been living!" To this I would reply, "Gentlemen, all the time you have been here listening you have also been deciding again and again what you were going to be. This has been one of the decisive hours of your life, but it has been relatively passive because you have been listeners. Yet this falls directly within my definition. Here is the proof: while you were listening to me, some of you have more than once wavered between ceasing to pay attention to me and continuing generously to listen, alert to what I was saying. You have decided on one course or the other —to be attentive or to be distracted, to think about this subject or another one—and that, thinking about life or about something else, is what your life is *now*. The same thing applies to those who did not waver, who stayed firmly resolved to hear me to the end. Moment by moment, again and again, they have had to feed this resolution in order to keep it alive, so that they could continue to be attentive. Even the firmest of our decisions must constantly be receiving corroboration, must constantly be renewed, freshly charged like a gun whose powder loses force with lack of use; in short, must be re-decided. When you came here you had decided what you were going to be; you would be listeners; once here, you re-iterated this proposal again and again—otherwise you would have escaped little by little from between the cruel hands of the orator."

And now let us look at the immediate consequence of all this: if life consists in deciding what we are going to be, this means that at the very root and base of our lives there is a temporal attribute. To decide what we are going to be means to take account of the future. And now we are getting a whole fruitful harvest of discoveries. First we find that our life is a constant series of collisions with the future. Here is another paradox. In the process of living, neither the present nor the past comes first.

Life is an activity executed in relation to the future; we find the present or the past afterwards, in relation to that future. Life is what comes next, what has not yet come to pass.

11

The Basic Reality Is Our Life. The Categories of Life. Theoretic Life. Destiny and Freedom.

WHENEVER I have said that we were seeing ourselves forced to move beyond the boundaries of antiquity and modernity, I have added that we go beyond them only insofar as we conserve them. The spirit, by its very essence, is at once most cruel, most tender, and most generous. In order to live, the spirit must murder its own past, thus denying it, but this it cannot do without at the same time reviving the thing it kills and keeping it alive within itself. If it kills once and for all, it could not go on denying that past, and because it denies it, superseding it. If our thought did not re-think the thought of Descartes, and if Descartes did not re-think the thought of Aristotle, ours would be primitive; we would no longer be the heirs of what has gone before, but would have to go back and begin again. To surpass is to inherit and to add to.

When I say that we need new concepts I refer to all that we must add to what already exists—the old concepts endure, but they become subordinate. If we discover a new manner of being which is more fundamental than the old, it is evident that we need a concept of being which was previously unknown—but at the same time our newest concept has the obligation to explain the old ones, it must demonstrate that portion of truth which they contained. Thus we suggested some days ago (there was no time to do more than hint) how the old idea of cosmic being and the substantive self had value for a reality in which the most basic fact of consciousness had not yet been discovered, and later we showed how the concept of the subjective being would be valid if there were not a previous reality which is life itself.

Well then, antiquity and modernity coincide in seeking, under the name of philosophy, a knowledge of the Universe, or whatever there is. But on taking the first step, on seeking the first truth about the Universe, the two of them begin to draw apart. The ancient starts off in search of primary reality, understanding by primary that reality which is most important in the structure of the Universe. If this reality is theist, this means that the most important reality, the one which explains the rest, is God: if it is materialist, the most important will be matter; if pantheist, it will be an undifferentiated entity, at once God and matter—*natura sive Deus*. But the modern will hold up all this searching and will dispute it, saying, "It is possible that this reality or that may, in fact, be the most important in the Universe, but even after we have demonstrated this we will be not one step further ahead because you have forgotten to ask yourselves whether that reality which explains all the rest is a reality with full evidence; and more, whether those other less important realities which it explains are realities that exist beyond the shadow of a doubt."

The first problem of philosophy is not one of finding out which reality in the Universe is the most important, but which is the most sure, the one beyond any trace of doubt, even though it be perhaps the least important, the most humble and insignificant. In short, the primary philosophic problem consists in determining what of the Universe is given to us, the problem of fundamental data. The ancients never posed this problem formally; hence, whatever their skill in regard to the other questions, their level is below the level of modernity. So we install ourselves on this level, and the only thing we do is to dispute with the moderns about which reality is fundamental and indubitable. We find that it is not the conscious self, the subject, but life which includes both the subject and the world. In this way we escape from idealism and win to a new level.

But note that we do all this without departing from philosophy's first problem, that we move exclusively on the plane of what, among all there is, has been given to us. If we believe that this datum is our own life, that of all the Universe what is given to each of us is only his own life, we do not allow ourselves the slightest opinion on the question as to whether, in addition to what is given us, there are not other realities which, though not given us, are much more important. The problem of that which is given or indubitable is not philosophy but only its doorstep, its preliminary chapter. I want to remind you that this was said in the beginning.

But I do not know whether you have all noted the consequence that this statement carries with it; this is an elemental consequence, so elemental that, strictly speaking, I ought not to voice it, but I fear it should be stated. It is this: if we have recognized that the only indubitable reality is as we have already defined it, nothing else that we may say will ever be able to contradict the attributes which, with all evidence, make up that basic reality. Because all the other things of which we speak, different from that primordial thing, are doubtful and secondary, and firm only insofar as they rest on that reality which is beyond doubt.

Suppose, for example, that someone starts from the modern principle and says that the only thing which is beyond doubt is the existence of thought—with this statement he takes his stand on the level that we call modernity. But then he adds: of course in addition there is matter, the matter which physics knows, composed of atoms ruled by certain laws. If by that "in addition there is" he means that what physics says has the same operative rank as the principle of subjectivism, the statement is utterly absurd. This principle says that the indubitable real is nonmaterial and that for it the rules of physics (a science which, like every individual science, occupies itself with secondary and quasi-realities) have no force. This is not to deny the truth of physical laws, but to relegate their operative force to the secondary order of phenomena which they concern; the order of phenomena which do not pretend to be basic. The idealist physicist, that is to say, the modern one, like the idealist philosopher, will have to explain how, if there is no other indubitable reality than thought, which is nonmaterial, one can talk with good sense and truth about material things, about physical laws and so on—but what he cannot do sensibly is to let physics exercise retroactive effects on the definition of that reality which is beyond doubt.

This definition is something not to be touched, and not to be destroyed by what, using it as a point of departure, we will add later. This is the elemental thing which I suspect it would be not inopportune to emphasize.

The new fact, the new fundamental reality, is "our life," the life of every one of us. Let anyone try to talk of any other reality as being freer from doubt, more primary than this, and you will see that such a thing is impossible. Even thinking is not anterior to living—because thinking is found to be a piece of my life, a particular act in that life. This seeking for an indubitable reality is something that I do because I live and inasmuch as I live —that is to say, it is not isolated and done for its own sake. I seek reality because I am now busying myself with philosophy, and I do this as a first act in philosophizing. And philosophizing is, in turn, a particular form of living which assumes this living—for if I work with philosophy it is because of an earlier desire to know what the Universe is, and this curiosity, in turn, exists because of what I feel as a desire of my life which is restless about itself, and perhaps finds itself lost in itself. In short, whatever reality we set up as primary, we find that it assumes our life to be a fact; the act of giving it place is in itself a vital act, is "living."

It may seem very surprising that the only indubitable reality should be "living" and not thinking—the idealist "*cogito*" (which in turn was very surprising in its day), or Aristotle's "form," or Plato's "idea," each of which in its own moment seemed an intolerable paradox. But what can we do? This is the way it is.

But if it is thus, there is no remedy but to fix the attributes of that new fundamental reality, and no remedy but to accept them even though they may seem to give the lie to all our pre-existent theories and to all the other science we follow, while recognizing them as true at certain points. In a system of philosophy, we would, then, have to show how, taking the reality of our life as a point of departure, and without contradicting our concept of living at a single point, there are also organic bodies, moral and physical laws, and even theology. But what I say does not include any statement that in addition

to that indubitable life of ours—that life which is given
to us—there may not perhaps exist the "other life."
What is certain is that that "other life" is, from the point
of view of science, problematical, as are organic reality
and physical reality—and that, on the other hand, this life
of ours, this life of every one of us, is not problematical
but indubitable.

Earlier, we began the definition of life in the rapid
form which haste demands. You may feel disturbed because what we were saying was something of a platitude.
But this means that it was evident, and we are clinging
to evidence. Life is not a mystery, but quite the opposite;
it is the clearest and most present thing there is, and being so, being purely transparent, we find difficulty in
studying it closely. The eye goes beyond it, toward wis-
doms that are still problematical, and it is an effort for us
to stop it at these immediate evidences.

Thus it is obvious that to live is to find myself in the
world. If I should suddenly find myself alone with myself, I would be existing, but that existing would not be
living—it would be merely the subjective existence of
idealism. But the fact is that I should not find myself
alone with myself, for when I explore that self I find it
to consist of a person who is occupied with something
which is not the self, with other things that show themselves united as if articulated among themselves; these
face me in the shape of my surroundings as an enveloping
unity of a world where I exist—and I am here not passively, not prone and inert, but under pressure by that
world or exalted by it.

The world is what I find confronting and surrounding
me when I find myself, the thing that clearly exists for
me and acts upon me. The world is not the same as
nature, not the same as that cosmos familiar to the an-

cients, which was an underlying reality subsisting by itself, a reality of which its subjects may know this bit or
that, but which reserves to itself its own mystery. The
vital, living world has no mystery at all for me, because
it consists exclusively of what I observe in it and just as
I observe it. Nothing intervenes in my life except what
presents itself to me. In short, the world is what is lived,
as it is lived. Let us suppose that my world were composed of pure mysteries, of things that were masked and
enigmatic, like the world in certain American films. Well
then, that fact that they were mysteries, were enigmas,
would be evident and transparent to me, would act on
me in the shape of mystery and enigma; I would then
have to say that the world in which I live is an evident
and indubitable mystery, its self is clearly composed of
the mysterious; and all this would be as simple as though
I said that the world is blue or is yellow.

The primary attribute of this basic reality which we
call "our life" is the fact of existing on one's own account,
of entering into an understanding of oneself, of being
transparent to oneself. Only thus is it, and whatever forms
part of it, indubitable—and only because it is the
uniquely indubitable is it the fundamental reality.

This "finding oneself," this "understanding oneself,"
this "being transparent," is the first category of living.
Some of you do not know what a category is. Do not
be ashamed. A category is an elemental thing in philosophic science. Do not be ashamed at ignorance of a thing
that is elemental. All of us are ignorant of elemental
things which our neighbors know all too well. The
shameful thing is not ignorance—on the contrary, that
is the natural thing. The really shameful thing is to not
want to know, to resist finding out when the occasion
offers. It is never the ignorant who offer that resistance,

but the ones who think they know. That is the shameful thing—to think you know. He who thinks he knows something, but is in fact ignorant of it, closes the door of his mind through which authentic truth could enter. His own dull idea, held proudly or stubbornly, acts as does the guard among the termites—a type with an enormous head, varnished and very hard, dedicated to the duty of standing in the entrance to the nest, blocking the orifice with its own head so that nothing can enter. In the same way he who believes that he knows something uses his own head to close the mental trap door through which true knowledge might enter.

Anyone who has carried on an active and public intellectual life, within Spain and without, will automatically make comparisons; he is forced to the conviction that this mental attitude of being hermetically sealed is in the Spaniard a permanent and endemic vice. And this is not chance. If the Spaniard shows very little intellectual porosity, it is because he also is a hermit in zones of his soul which go much deeper than intellect. But perhaps even graver than this lack of porosity on the part of the Spanish man is that same weakness in the soul of the Spanish woman. To say this is to commit an atrocity, but I do not do it carelessly. As soon as words can circulate freely, I shall begin a campaign against the Spanish woman's way of living. It will not be flattering, and for me it will be very painful.

I have always been repelled by the person who is continually saying that he believes that this, that, or the other thing ought to be done. During my lifetime I have thought of myself very seldom in terms of duty. I have lived my life, and I continue to live it, pushed almost entirely not by duties, but by illusions. More than that; the ethics which I may be able to set before you in the coming year differs from traditional ethics in that it considers the primary idea in morality to be not duty but illusion. Duty is important, but it is a secondary thing—it is the substitute for, the *ersatz* of illusion. What we cannot manage to achieve out of illusion we must at least do out of a sense of duty.

Well, then, this campaign, on the theme of the Spanish woman, is too harsh to be an illusion; on the contrary, it will be a sacrifice. For many years of meditation I have believed it to be a duty. Of all the things in our Spanish life which need basic reform I think the one most fundamentally in need of it is the feminine soul. And for one who believes, as I do, that woman intervenes in history infinitely more than is generally believed or suspected, and that she does this in continuous, irresistible and most subtle ways, it is clear as crystal that no small number of capital defects, persistent throughout Spanish existence, of which the origin is sought in the most abstruse causes, arise simply out of the inadequacy of Spanish femininity. Difficult and dangerous though it may be, and although I can foresee the uncomfortable consequences which it will bring for me, I feel obliged to take this task upon myself.

As you see, at this point, too, I depart absolutely from the official stereotypes. I am hardly gallant, but one must lay all gallantry aside, must overcome it along with the modernity and idealism which made up its climate—one must move ahead to forms of enthusiasm about women which are much more difficult, energetic and ardent. Nothing today seems more untimely than the devoted and curving gesture with which the lordly gentleman of 1890 approached a woman to address her with a phrase that was as gallant and curled as a shaving. Young girls are losing the habit of being addressed with gallantry, and that gesture which thirty years ago oozed virility in every pore would today seem to them a bit effeminate.

But let us go back to our subject, which was the matter of categories. We were saying that some of you neither had, nor had any reason for having, a clear idea of what categories are. The idea of the category is the simplest in the world. A horse and a star differ in many of their elements and in the major part of their ingredients. But however different they are, they have something in common when we say of them that they are both corporeal things. The horse and the star are both real things; moreover they both occupy space, they exist in time, they suffer changes in the course of moving about, and in turn they produce changes in other things on colliding with them; each has its own color, form and density, that is to say, its own qualities. Thus we find that over and above their innumerable differences they coincide in a small number of elements and attributes—being real, occupying space and time, having qualities, acting and suffering. Like them, everything which pretends to be a corporeal thing will possess that minimal group of conditions or properties, that essential skeleton of the corporeal being. Well then, these are the categories as Aristotle defined them. The properties which every real being, simply by the fact of being real, carries with it and contains, quite apart from other elements which differentiate it.

As our reality, "living," is very different from the ancient cosmic reality, it will be made up of a group of categories or components, all of them essential, equally original and inseparable among themselves. It is these categories of "our life" that we seek. Our life is the life of "each one of us"; therefore mine is different from yours, but both of them are "my living," and both of them will have a series of common ingredients—the categories of "my life." Nevertheless, there is a radical difference between the reality called "my life" and the reality which the older philosophy called "being." "Being" is a general thing which does not pretend in itself to be the character of the individual. The Aristotelian categories are categories of being in general—ὄν ἧ ὄν. But "my life" is different; whether this name is applied in my case, or to any one of you, it is a concept which then involves the individual; hence we have found one of those very rare ideas which is equally "general" and "individual." Up to now, logic has ignored the possibility of a concept which in appearance is so contradictory. Hegel himself, who wanted to search for something similar, did not succeed; his "concrete universal" is in the last analysis universal, but not truly and fundamentally concrete; it is not individual. But I cannot even start now to go into this theme. Let us move ahead, leaving the windward beat as it was.

The first category of our lives is "to find oneself," "to understand oneself," "to be transparent," and once more I want to warn you not to forget that here it is not merely the self which is the subject, but also the world. I take account of myself in the world, of myself and the world, that is to say, I live.

But this "to find oneself" is, after all, to find oneself occupied with something in the world. I consist in an occupying of myself with what there is in the world, and the world consists of everything with which I occupy myself, and of nothing else. To occupy oneself is to do this or that—it is, for example, to think. Thinking is living because it is occupying myself with objects in that peculiar dealing with them which is thinking them. To think is to make; for example, to create truths, to make a philosophy. To occupy oneself is to make a philosophy, or to make a revolution, to make a cigarette, to make a footing, to make time. This is what I am during my lifetime.

As for things, what are they? In this basic perspective and primary mode of thinking which is their being lived by me, what are they? I am he who makes—who thinks, runs, rebels, or hopes—and what is the thing that is made?

Curious! That which is made is also my life. When what I do is to wait, the thing which is done is the act of having waited; when what I make is the cigarette, the thing done is not, properly speaking, the cigarette, but my action in rolling it. In itself and apart from my activity, the cigarette has no primary being; this was the ancient error. The cigarette is what I manipulate in making it, and when I have finished my activity and the object of my rolling has ceased to be, it is converted into another object—it is that which someone must light and must then smoke. Its true being is reduced to what it represents as the object of my occupation. It has no being in itself, subsistent, χωριστόν, apart from my living it, my action with it. Its being is functional, its function in my life: it is a being *so that*, a being toward an end—so that I may do this or that with it. Nevertheless, as in traditional philosophy, I talk of the being of things as something which these things have by themselves and apart from their manipulation and their service in my life— I use the ancient meaning of the concept "to be"; the result is apparent when I abstract from a thing its primary being, which is the usual, serviceable, and lived being; then I find that the thing has not disappeared because I am not occupied with it, but that it remains apart, outside my life, perhaps in the hope that it may be of some service to me another time.

But then that thing which is in being on *its own ac-*

count, and not for reasons of my life, surges forth in virtue of my abstracting it from my life—and abstracting is also a doing, a making and an occupying oneself, it is occupying myself in pretending that I do not live, or at least that I do not live this thing or that, it is *putting* this apart from me. Therefore the manner in which things exist for themselves, their cosmic and subsistent being, is also a being *for* me; it is what they are when I leave off living them, when I pretend not to live them. This attitude of pretense (which is not to say that it is insincere or false, but only possessed of certain attributes of its own) in which I assume that I do not exist, and therefore that I do not see things as they are for me, and ask myself how they will then be, this attitude of virtual nonliving is the theoretic attitude.

Do you see how Fichte continues to be right, and theorizing, philosophizing are, properly speaking, not living—precisely because they are a form of living; *the theoretic life, the contemplative life?* Theory, and its extreme form, philosophy, are the attempt which life makes to transcend itself; it is to de-occupy oneself, to de-live, to cease to be interested in things. But this dis-interesting of oneself is not a passive process. On the contrary, it is a form of being interested: for instance, to be interested in something while cutting the intro-vital threads which link it to me—saving it from its immersion in my life, leaving it alone, in pure reference to its own self, seeking in it its very being. To be dis-interested is, then, to be interested in the inner self of each individual thing, to dower it with independence, with substance, one might almost say with personality—putting myself in a position to look at it from within its own point of view, not from mine. Contemplation is an attempt at transmigration. But that—to seek in a thing what it has of the absolute and to cut off all other partial interest of my own toward it, to cease to make use of it, to cease to wish that it serves me, but to serve it myself as an impartial eye so that it may see itself and find itself and be its very own self and for itself—this—this—is this not love? Then is contemplation, at root, an act of love, in that in loving, as differentiated from desiring, we are trying to live from within the other and we un-live ourselves for the sake of the other? The old and divine Plato, whom we deny, continues generously to encourage and cheer us in our denial, nourishing it, inspiring it and giving it flavor. Thus we find his idea about the erotic origin of knowledge in a form which is certainly new and different.

I have touched this point headlong, without purifying or analyzing any of the expressions employed, so that in this short and crude form you may glimpse where the traditional meaning of being will appear in this new philosophy; and incidentally, so that you may see what our path would have been if time had not been lacking. To the question, "What is philosophy?" we would have responded more from the root up than has ever been done up to now. Earlier we defined what philosophic doctrine is and we have progressed to the point where we met life—but now we have reached the point where we are really going to answer our question. Because the philosophic doctrine, as it is or can be in books, is only the abstraction of the authentic reality which is philosophy—is only its precipitate, its semi-moribund body. As the concrete, not the abstract, reality of the cigarette is what the smoker will go on rolling, so philosophy's self is what the philosopher makes it; philosophizing is a form of living. And this is what I would like to have investigated most carefully in your company. What is philosophizing as a form of living? We have seen vaguely that it is a de-living, a de-living for whatever there is, for the Universe—a making of oneself a place where the Universe is known and recognized. But it is useless, without long analysis, to try to give those words all their strict and fruitful meaning. Let me rest content with remembering that the Greeks, having no books which could properly be called philosophic, when asked by someone like Plato, "What is philosophy?"—thought of man, of the philosopher, of life. For them, philosophizing was first of all βίος δεωρητιχός, a theory of life. Strictly speaking, the first philosophic books which they had were books of the lives of the seven sages, biographies. All that which does not define philosophy as philosophizing, and philosophizing as an essential type of life, is neither sufficient nor basic.

But before concluding, I would like to carry the definition of "our life" a bit further. We have seen that it is finding oneself occupied with this or that, a form of doing or making. But all doing is a process of occupying oneself with something and for something. The occupation which is now an expression of ourselves is rooted in and directed toward what is commonly called an end. That "toward" in view of which I now do this, and in so doing live and have my being, I chose because among the possibilities which lay before me I believed that my life would be better if I occupied myself this way.

Each of these words is a category, and as such, an analysis of it would be inexhaustible. Out of them comes my actual life, the life I make, or what I actually do, the life that I decided upon: that is to say, before my life as I make it comes a process of deciding to make it—of deciding my life. Our life decides itself, anticipating itself. It is not given to us ready-made—not like the trajectory of the bullet to which I referred earlier. But it consists in deciding, because living is finding oneself in a world which, by no means hermetically sealed, is always offering opportunities. For me the vital world, every instant of it, is composed of being able to do this or that, not of having perforce to do this and only this.

On the other hand, these possibilities are not unlimited —if they were, they would not be concrete possibilities but a purely indeterminate collection, and in a world of absolute indetermination, in which everything is equally possible, it is not possible to decide on anything. In order that there may be decision there must be both space and limitation, relative determination. This I express in the category called "circumstances." Life always finds itself amid certain circumstances, in an arrangement surrounding it, filled with things and other people. One does not live in a world which is vague; constitutionally the vital world is circumstance, the things and the people about one, this world, here and now. And circumstance is something determined, closed, but at the same time open and with internal latitude, with space or emptiness in which to move about and to make one's decisions; circumstance is a riverbed which life goes on cutting within a valley from which it cannot escape. To live is to live here, now; the here and the now are specific, not to be exchanged for others, but they are ample.

All life is a constant process of deciding between various possibilities. *Astra inclinant, non trahunt*—the stars impel, but they do not compel. Life is at the same time freedom and fatality; it is being free within a given destiny. This fate offers us a determined and inexorable repertory of possibilities, that is to say, it offers us different destinies. We accept the fatality and within it we decide on a destiny. Life is destiny.

I hope that no one of you will think it necessary to

warn me that determinism denies liberty. I would answer that I am sorry both for determinism and for him. To put the best face on determinism, it is, or rather it was, a theory about the reality of the Universe. Although it was certain, it was no more than a theory, an interpretation, a consciously problematical thesis which had to be proven. Therefore, even though I were a determinist, I could not let that theory exercise retroactive effects on the primary and indubitable reality which we are now describing. However deterministic the determinist may be, his living as such is relatively undetermined, and at one specific moment he made his decision between determinism and indeterminism. Thus to present that question here would be not to know what determinism is, or what is the analysis of primordial reality prior to every theory.

And do not overlook the fact that when I say life is at one and the same time fate and freedom, a possibility that though limited is still a possibility and therefore open —do not fail to note what I am saying. I myself can not reason about it, that is to say, prove it, nor do I have to reason it out—more than that, I consciously flee from all reasoning and limit myself purely to expressing myself in concepts, to describing the basic reality which I have before me and which is assumed in every theory in all reasoning and in every proof. It was in order to forestall sad observations like that one, which I prefer not to assume in you, that I made that overly elementary observation in the beginning.

And now, parenthetically, may I note that the determinist theory as such has no existence today either in philosophy or in physics. Solid support for that statement is to be found in a sentence by one of the best modern physicists, the successor of Einstein, Hermann Weyl; in a book on the logic of physics which was published a few years ago he said, "From all the aforesaid one can judge how far is physics today—composed half of laws and half of statistics—from a position in which it could venture forth to undertake the defense of determinism." One of the mechanisms of the mental hermetism to which he alludes is that when we hear something and a very elemental objection occurs to us, we seldom think that this may also have occurred to the one who is speaking or writing, and that the truth may be that we have not understood what he has been saying. If we fail to think this, we will remain on a level lower than the person we are listening to, or the book we are reading.

So life is that paradoxical reality which consists in deciding what we are going to do, therefore in being what we not yet are, in starting to be the future. Contrary to the ways of cosmic being, the living being begins by being the creature over there, the one that comes afterwards.

This would be impossible if time were originally cosmic time. Cosmic time is only the present, because the future has not yet come, and the past no longer is. How, then, can past and future continue to be part of time? This is what makes the concept of time so difficult that it troubles philosophers.

"Our life" is set and anchored in the immediate present. But what is my life at this moment? It is not the process of saying what I am saying; what I am living this moment is not a matter of moving the lips; that is mechanical, outside my life, it pertains to the cosmic being. On the contrary, my life is the process of thinking what I am going to say; at this moment I am anticipating, I am projecting myself into the future. But in order to say this I make use of certain means—of words—and that gives me a portion of my past. My future, then, makes me discover my past in order to realize that future. The past is now real because I am re-living it, and it is when I find in the past the means of realizing my future that I discover my present. And all this happens in an instant; moment by moment life swells out into the three dimensions of the true interior time. The future tosses me back toward the past; the past toward the present, and from here I go again toward the future which throws me back to the past, and the past to another present, in a constant rotation.

We are anchored in the cosmic present, which is like the ground which our feet press while body and head reach toward the future. Nicolas of Cusa was right when he said, at the dawn of the Renaissance, *Ita nunc sive praesens complicat tempus*. The now, the present, includes all time; now, before, and after.

We live in the present, at the actual point of it, but it does not exist primarily for us; out of it, as out of the earth, we live the immediate future.

Observe that of all the points of the earth the only one which we cannot directly perceive is that which lies beneath our feet.

Before we see what surrounds us we are originally a bundle of appetites, desires, and illusions. We come into the world dowered with a system of preferences and prejudices, more or less like those of our neighbors, which each of us carries within himself like a battery of sympathies and repulsions, ready to shoot them off in favor of this or against that. The heart, that tireless machine of preferring and disdaining, is the support of our personality.

Do not, then, say that the first thing is the impression. Nothing is more important in remaking the idea of what man is than to correct the traditional perspective according to which we are supposed to want a thing for the reason that we have seen it earlier. That may seem obvious, yet it is mostly an error. He who desires material riches did not wait to want them until he saw the gold; he would seek it wherever it could be found, giving his full attention to the business side that every situation holds within itself. The artist, on the other hand, the man of esthetic preferences, will go through those same situations utterly blind to their economic side and will seek whatever there is in them of grace and beauty.

Hence the traditional belief must be turned upside down. We do not desire a thing because we have first seen it; on the contrary, we go seeking it throughout the world because in our heart of hearts we would prefer that kind of thing. Of all the sounds which are continually assaulting us and which we could hear if we tried, we hear only those to which we give our attention; that is to say, those which we favor with a special ear. And as we cannot attend to one thing without subtracting attention from another, what we do when we hear one sound that interests us is to dis-hear all the others. All seeing is a process of looking at, all hearing is in the last analysis a listening-to, all living is an incessant, original preferring and disdaining.

Nowhere, perhaps, is this clearer than in the delicate area of our love affairs. In the slumbering depth of the feminine soul, woman, when truly a woman, is always the sleeping beauty, waiting amid life's forest to be awakened by the kiss of the prince. In the depth of her soul she bears, unknowing, the pre-formed image of a man—not an individual image of an individual man, but a generic type of masculine perfection. And, always asleep, she moves like a sleepwalker among the men she meets, contrasting their physical and moral figures with that of her pre-existent and preferred model.

This explains two events which occur in every authentic love affair. One is the suddenness of falling in love: the woman, and the same is true of the man, finds herself suddenly, without process or transition, aflame with love. This would be inexplicable if the casual contact with this particular man had not been preceded by a secret and tacit surrender of her being to that model of a man which she has always carried within herself. The other fact is the way in which the woman, on finding herself deeply in love, not only feels that her love will be eternal, and for all future time, but seems to herself to have loved this man forever, out of the mysterious depths of the past, from time beyond measure and untold epochs of previous existence.

This eternal, and as it were, innate devotion clearly does not stem from the individual who has just appeared upon her horizon, but from that interior ideal of a man which throbbed like a promise in the depth of her quiet soul and who now, in this real being, has found realization and fulfillment.

In this extreme measure and up to such a point is human living a constant anticipation, a pre-forming of the future. We are always very perspicacious with regard to those things in which the qualities that we prefer are realized; on the other hand, we are blind to those which, though of equal or even superior perfections, belong to a type of thing that is foreign to our innate sensibility. The future comes first: incessantly we press it with eager attention so that its favorable juices may drip into our hands; and only in terms of what we demand of it, what we hope of it, do we turn our eyes toward the present and the past in order to find within them the means with which to satisfy our desires. The future is always the leader, the *Dux:* the present and the past are always aides-de-camp and soldiers. We live moving forward into our future, supported by the present, with the past, always faithful, off to the edge, a little sad, a little frail, as the moon, lighting a path through the night, goes with us step by step, shedding its pale friendship on our shoulders.

Psychologically, then, the decisive thing is not the sum of what we have been, but of what we yearn to be: the appetite, the desire, the illusion, the ambition. Whether we like it or not, our life is in its very essence futurism. Man goes being carried *du bout du nez* by his illusion—a baroque and picturesque image which is justified because the end of man's nose is, in fact, what usually goes ahead; it is the part of us which goes into the spatial "over there," the thing that anticipates and precedes us.

The process of deciding on this or that is a portion of our lives which has about it a certain breath of freedom. We are constantly deciding our future being, and to realize it we must count on the past and make use of the present as it operates on the actuality, and all of this within the "now"; because that future is not just any future, but the possible "now," and that past is not the past of someone who lived a hundred years ago, but the past up to now. Do you see? "Now" is our time, our world, our life. This flows along calm or tumultuous, a river or a torrent, through the landscape of actuality, of that unique actuality, world, and time to which we give a number, as of years after Jesus Christ. In it we go encrusted; it marks out for us an entire repertory of possibilities, of conditions, dangers, means and facilities. With its features it limits the freedom of decision which motivates our life, and in the face of that freedom it becomes our destiny.

To say that our times form our destiny is not merely a phrase. The present, in which the past—the individual and the historic past—is summarized and condensed, is that portion of fate which intervenes in our life; in this sense life always carries a fatal dimension and some hint of having fallen into a trap. Except that this trap does not strangle us, but leaves to life a margin of decision and always permits us, out of the imposed situation, to achieve an elegant solution and to forge for ourselves a beautiful life. Hence, because life is part fate, and part the freedom we need to make decisions for ourselves, there is at its very root the stuff of art; nothing symbolizes this better than the position of the poet who bases his lyric freedom on the exigencies of rhyme and rhythm. All art implies the acceptance of a shackle, of a destiny; as Nietzsche said, "The artist is he who dances in chains." The destiny which is the present is not a misfortune but a delight, the delight that the chisel feels when it encounters the resistance of the marble.

Imagine for a moment that each one of us takes only a little more care for each hour of his days, that he demands in it a little more of elegance and intensity; then, multiplying all these minute pressures toward the perfecting and deepening of each life by all the others, calculate for yourselves the gigantic enrichment, the fabulous ennobling which this process would create for human society.

This would be living at the top of one's form; instead of drifting through hours that pass like rudderless ships, we would find them moving before us, each with its new imminence and importance.

And do not say that fate does not allow us to improve

our lives, for the beauty of life does not lie in the fact that destiny is or is not favorable to us, but in the grace with which we accept the challenge and out of its fatal material fashion a noble figure.

But let us gather into one clear formula our entire analysis of what, in its fundamental essence, our life is. These perceptions of fundamental facts flee one's comprehension like shy birds—and it helps to shut them into a cage fashioned from an expressive name which lets us see between the wires the idea made prisoner.

We have seen that living consists in the process of deciding what we are going to be. Heidegger says very delicately, "then life is concern"—*Sorge*—what the Latins call *cura*, from whence comes cure, procure, curiosity, and so on. In ancient Spanish the word "cuidar" (to care for, to take care) had precisely the meaning which we now find in such terms as curator, procurator, curate of souls. But I prefer to express a similar, although not identical, idea with a word which seems to me more exact: I say that life is preoccupation, and not only in moments which are difficult, but all the time; in essence it is no more than this, to be preoccupied. Every moment of the day we are having to decide what we are going to do the next moment, what it is that will occupy our lives. This is occupying ourselves in anticipation, pre-occupying ourselves.

But perhaps someone, reluctant to surrender a vigilant habit of mind, objects thus—"Sir, this is a play on words. I admit that life consists in deciding moment by moment what we are going to do, but the word preoccupation has, in the common phrase, a sense that always suggests an anxious, a difficult moment; to be preoccupied with something is to make a very serious question of it. But when we decided to come here, to spend this space of time in this fashion, there is no use pretending that we made a great question out of it. On the contrary, as you said, most of life flows by without our paying it undue attention. Why, then, use a word which is so grave, so full of pathos, if it does not coincide with what it is supposed to describe? We are no longer, fortunately, under the reign of romanticism, which fed on exaggeration and impropriety. We demand that one speak with simplicity, clarity and exactness, in words as fresh and disinfected as a surgeon's instruments."

I do not know why I assume that any one of you would make such an objection. It is, in fact, a skillful objection, and for one who is by vocation an intellectual —I pretend to nothing else, and this I am with passion— to such a one, skillful objections are the most agreeable things in the world; as an intellectual I have come into this world for no other reason but to make and to receive objections. Thus I receive them with delight, I not only receive them but I esteem them, not only do I esteem them but I solicit them. Always I know how to extract from them an excellent profit. If we go on tossing them back and forth they allot us the pleasure of victory and we can make the triumphant gesture of the good bowman who has put an arrow into the bull's-eye. If, on the contrary, the objection defeats us and even convinces us, what better fortune? It is the voluptuous pleasure of the convalescent, the awakening from a nightmare; we have given birth to a new truth and, reflecting this new-born light, the pupil widens. Therefore I accept the objection: cleanness, clarity, exactness, are the divinities to whom I, too, dedicate a trembling worship.

But it is also clear that as I have been attacked, though the attack be imaginary, I must defend myself with weapons that are effective; if I am sure that they are clean, I am not so sure that they may not also include a certain roughness.

Hypothetically, then, we are left with the assumption that some of you have come here without preoccupying yourself with what you did, without questioning it. Nothing happens more frequently, and if certain suspicions of the psychologist did not dissuade us from leaning on appearances, we would have to believe that the normal form of life is lack of preoccupation. But then, if you did not come here for a special reason of your own, because of something which preoccupied you, why did you come? The reply is inevitable—because others came.

Here is the whole secret of failure to be preoccupied. When we believe ourselves not to be preoccupied with life, we let that life float rudderless, like a buoy without anchor chains, coming and going as it is pushed by social currents. And this is what makes man common and woman mediocre, that is to say, what puts them in with the vast majority of human beings. For them, to live is to surrender to the unanimous, to let customs, prejudices, habits, topics, be installed within them, give them life, and take on the task of making them live. They are weak animals which, on sensing the weight of their own lives at a moment either dolorous or delightful, feel themselves apprehensive, and then eager to free their shoulders from the very weight which is their being and throw it on the collective group: that is to say, they are preoccupied with becoming un-preoccupied. Under their apparent indifference throbs a secret fear of having to solve for themselves the problems posed by their acts and emotions—a humble desire to be like everybody else, to renounce the responsibility of their own destiny, and dissolve it amid the multitude. This is the eternal ideal

of the weak, whose preoccupation it is to do what everyone else is doing.

And if we seek an image akin to that of the eye of
Horus, let us remember the rite of Egyptian burials, of
that people who believed that on the other side of the
grave man was summoned before a court. In that tribunal
his life was judged: the first and supreme act of justice
was to find the weight of his heart. In order to avoid
this weighing, to deceive those powers of life and after-
life, the Egyptian had the burial squad replace the heart
of flesh and blood with one made out of bronze or of
black stone; he was trying to replace his life. This is
what the un-preoccupied try to do—to substitute for
their own being another one. This is what obsesses them.
Since there is no way to escape the essential condition of
living, and as living is reality, the best and most discreet
course is to emphasize it, to underline it with irony; this
was the elegant gesture of the fairy queen, Titania, who,
in Shakespeare's enchanted forest, caressed the head of
a donkey.

In the way of priests everywhere, Japanese priests
curse all that is earthly, and in describing the restless
futility of our world, they call it a "world of mist." In
one of their poets, Isa, there appears a simple *"hai-kai"*
which has stayed in my mind, and this is what it says,
"A world of mist is no more than a world of mist . . .
and yet . . ." And yet . . . let us accept that world of
mist as the material out of which to make a life that is
more complete.